REPORT OF A WORKSHOP ON THE SCOPE AND NATURE OF
COMPUTATIONAL THINKING

Committee for the Workshops on Computational Thinking

Computer Science and Telecommunications Board

Division on Engineering and Physical Sciences

NATIONAL RESEARCH COUNCIL
OF THE NATIONAL ACADEMIES

THE NATIONAL ACADEMIES PRESS
Washington, D.C.
www.nap.edu

THE NATIONAL ACADEMIES PRESS   500 Fifth Street, N.W.   Washington, DC 20001

NOTICE: The project that is the subject of this report was approved by the Governing Board of the National Research Council, whose members are drawn from the councils of the National Academy of Sciences, the National Academy of Engineering, and the Institute of Medicine. The members of the committee responsible for the report were chosen for their special competences and with regard for appropriate balance.

Support for this project was provided by the National Science Foundation under sponsor award number CNS-0831827. Any opinions expressed in this material are those of the authors and do not necessarily reflect the views of the agencies and organizations that provided support for the project.

International Standard Book Number-13:   978-0-309-14957-0
International Standard Book Number-10:   0-309-14957-6

Available at https://www.nap.edu.

Copyright 2010 by the National Academy of Sciences. All rights reserved.

Printed in the United States of America

THE NATIONAL ACADEMIES
Advisers to the Nation on Science, Engineering, and Medicine

The **National Academy of Sciences** is a private, nonprofit, self-perpetuating society of distinguished scholars engaged in scientific and engineering research, dedicated to the furtherance of science and technology and to their use for the general welfare. Upon the authority of the charter granted to it by the Congress in 1863, the Academy has a mandate that requires it to advise the federal government on scientific and technical matters. Dr. Ralph J. Cicerone is president of the National Academy of Sciences.

The **National Academy of Engineering** was established in 1964, under the charter of the National Academy of Sciences, as a parallel organization of outstanding engineers. It is autonomous in its administration and in the selection of its members, sharing with the National Academy of Sciences the responsibility for advising the federal government. The National Academy of Engineering also sponsors engineering programs aimed at meeting national needs, encourages education and research, and recognizes the superior achievements of engineers. Dr. Charles M. Vest is president of the National Academy of Engineering.

The **Institute of Medicine** was established in 1970 by the National Academy of Sciences to secure the services of eminent members of appropriate professions in the examination of policy matters pertaining to the health of the public. The Institute acts under the responsibility given to the National Academy of Sciences by its congressional charter to be an adviser to the federal government and, upon its own initiative, to identify issues of medical care, research, and education. Dr. Harvey V. Fineberg is president of the Institute of Medicine.

The **National Research Council** was organized by the National Academy of Sciences in 1916 to associate the broad community of science and technology with the Academy's purposes of furthering knowledge and advising the federal government. Functioning in accordance with general policies determined by the Academy, the Council has become the principal operating agency of both the National Academy of Sciences and the National Academy of Engineering in providing services to the government, the public, and the scientific and engineering communities. The Council is administered jointly by both Academies and the Institute of Medicine. Dr. Ralph J. Cicerone and Dr. Charles M. Vest are chair and vice chair, respectively, of the National Research Council.

www.national-academies.org

COMMITTEE FOR THE WORKSHOPS ON COMPUTATIONAL THINKING

MARCIA C. LINN, University of California, Berkeley, *Chair*
ALFRED V. AHO (NAE), Columbia University
M. BRIAN BLAKE, University of Notre Dame
ROBERT CONSTABLE, Cornell University
YASMIN B. KAFAI, University of Pennsylvania
JANET L. KOLODNER, Georgia Institute of Technology
LAWRENCE SNYDER, University of Washington, Seattle
URI WILENSKY, Northwestern University

Staff

HERBERT S. LIN, Study Director and Chief Scientist, CSTB
ENITA A. WILLIAMS, Associate Program Officer
SHENAE BRADLEY, Senior Program Assistant

COMPUTER SCIENCE AND TELECOMMUNICATIONS BOARD

ROBERT F. SPROULL, Sun Microsystems, Inc., *Chair*
PRITHVIRAJ BANERJEE, Hewlett Packard Company
WILLIAM J. DALLY, NVIDIA Corporation and Stanford University
DEBORAH ESTRIN, University of California
KEVIN KAHN, Intel Corporation, Hillsboro
JAMES KAJIYA, Microsoft Corporation
JOHN E. KELLY III, IBM
JON M. KLEINBERG, Cornell University
WILLIAM H. PRESS, University of Texas
PRABHAKAR RAGHAVAN, Yahoo! Research
DAVID E. SHAW, D.E. Shaw Research
ALFRED Z. SPECTOR, Google, Inc.
PETER SZOLOVITS, Massachusetts Institute of Technology
PETER J. WEINBERGER, Google, Inc.

JON EISENBERG, Director
RENEE HAWKINS, Financial and Administrative Manager
HERBERT S. LIN, Chief Scientist, CSTB
LYNETTE I. MILLETT, Senior Program Officer
NANCY GILLIS, Program Officer
ENITA A. WILLIAMS, Associate Program Officer
VIRGINIA BACON TALATI, Program Associate
SHENAE BRADLEY, Senior Program Assistant
ERIC WHITAKER, Senior Program Assistant

For more information on CSTB, see its website at http://www.cstb.org, write to CSTB, National Research Council, 500 Fifth Street, N.W., Washington, D.C. 20001, call (202) 334-2605, or e-mail the CSTB at cstb@nas.edu.

Preface

As the use of computational devices has become widespread, there is a need to understand the scope and impact of what is sometimes called the Information Revolution or the Age of Digital Information. This is particularly apparent in education at all levels. Various efforts have been made to introduce K-12 students to the most basic and essential computational concepts, and college curricula have tried to provide students a basis for lifelong learning of increasingly new and advanced computational concepts and technologies. At both ends of this spectrum, however, most efforts have not focused on fundamental concepts.

One common approach to incorporating computation into the K-12 curriculum is to emphasize computer literacy, which generally involves using tools to create newsletters, documents, Web pages, multimedia presentations, or budgets. A second common approach is to emphasize computer programming by teaching students to program in particular programming languages such as Java or C++. A third common approach focuses on programming applications such as games, robots, and simulations.

But in the view of many computer scientists, these three major approaches—although useful and arguably important—should not be confused with learning to think computationally. In this view, computational thinking is a fundamental analytical skill that everyone, not just computer scientists, can use to help solve problems, design systems, and understand human behavior. As such, they believe that computational thinking is comparable to the mathematical, linguistic, and logical reasoning that is taught to all children. This view mirrors the growing recognition that computational thinking (and not just computation) has begun to influence and shape thinking in many disciplines—Earth sciences, biology, and statistics, for example. Moreover, computational thinking is likely to benefit not only other scientists but also everyone else—bankers, stockbrokers, lawyers, car mechanics, salespeople, health care professionals, artists, and so on.

To explore these notions in greater depth, the Computer and Information Science and Engineering Directorate of the National Science Foundation asked the National Research Council (NRC) to conduct two workshops to explore the nature of computational thinking and its cognitive and educational implications. This report summarizes the first workshop, which focused on the scope and nature of computational thinking and on articulating what "computational thinking for everyone" might mean. A second workshop, to be held sometime later, will focus on the cognitive and educational dimensions of computational thinking.

Although this document was prepared by the Committee for the Workshops on Computational Thinking based on workshop presentations and discussions, it does not reflect consensus views of the committee. Under NRC guidelines for conducting workshops and developing report summaries, workshop activities do not seek consensus and workshop summaries (such as the present volume) cannot be said to represent "an NRC view" on the subject at hand. This workshop report reveals the plethora of perspectives on computational thinking, raises issues for the follow-on workshop concerned with pedagogy, and suggests the need for the field to build consensus on the scope, nature, and structure of computational thinking. The present report contains a digest of both presentations and discussion.

The workshop agenda and participants are described in Appendix A and Appendix B, respectively. Appendix C reprints the executive summary of the NRC's *Being Fluent with Information Technology* report (National Academy Press, Washington D.C., 1999). Appendix D provides an extended bibliography of additional references not contained in footnotes.

        Marcia C. Linn, *Chair*
        Committee for the Workshops on Computational Thinking

Acknowledgment of Reviewers

This report has been reviewed in draft form by individuals chosen for their diverse perspectives and technical expertise, in accordance with procedures approved by the National Research Council's (NRC's) Report Review Committee. The purpose of this independent review is to provide candid and critical comments that will assist the institution in making its published report as sound as possible and to ensure that the report meets institutional standards for objectivity, evidence, and responsiveness to the study charge. The review comments and draft manuscript remain confidential to protect the integrity of the deliberative process. We wish to thank the following individuals for their review of this report:

Edward A. Fox, Virginia Polytechnic Institute
Susanne Hambrusch, Purdue University
David E. Shaw, D.E. Shaw Research
Gerald Sussman, Massachusetts Institute of Technology
Ursula Wolz, The College of New Jersey
Wm. A. Wulf, University of Virginia

The reviewers listed above provided many constructive comments and suggestions; they did not see the final draft of the report before its release. The review of this report was coordinated by Harold Abelson of the Massachusetts Institute of Technology. Appointed by the NRC, he was responsible for making certain that an independent examination of this report was carried out in accordance with institutional procedures and that all review comments were carefully considered. Responsibility for the final content of this report rests entirely with the authoring committee and the institution.

Contents

1 INTRODUCTION 1
   1.1 Scope and Approach of This Report, 1
   1.2 Motivation—Why Should Anyone Care About Computational Thinking?, 3

2 WHAT IS COMPUTATIONAL THINKING? 7
   2.1 The Landscape of Computational Thinking, 8
   2.2 Computational Thinking as a Range of Concepts, Applications, Tools, and Skill Sets, 10
   2.3 Computational Thinking as Language and the Importance of Programming, 13
   2.4 Computational Thinking as the Automation of Abstractions, 16
   2.5 Computational Thinking as a Cognitive Tool, 17
   2.6 Computational Thinking in Contexts Without Programming a Computer, 20
   2.7 The Role of Computers and Technology, 26
   2.8 A Collaborative Dimension to Computational Thinking, 27
   2.9 What Computational Thinking Is Not, 28

3 LOOKING OUTWARD 33
   3.1 The Relationship of Computational Thinking to Mathematics and Engineering, 33
      3.1.1 Mathematical Thinking, 33
      3.1.2 Engineering, 34
   3.2 Disciplinary Applications of Computational Thinking, 36

    3.3 Computational Thinking Across Different Disciplines, 40
        3.3.1 Problem Solving/Debugging, 40
        3.3.2 Testing, 41
        3.3.3 Data Mining and Information Retrieval, 41
        3.3.4 Concurrency and Parallelism, 41
        3.3.5 Modeling, 42

4   RELATIONSHIP TO PAST AND ONGOING EFFORTS   45
    4.1 Previous Work, 45
        4.1.1 LOGO, 45
        4.1.2 Fluency with Information Technology (FIT), 46
        4.1.3 Computing the Future, 47
        4.1.4 Reflections on the Field, 51
        4.1.5 Engineering in K-12 Education, 52
        4.1.6 Technically Speaking, 53
    4.2 Some Drivers of Change, 54
        4.2.1 The National Science Foundation CPATH Program, 55
        4.2.2 The Computing Research Association Education Committee, 55
        4.2.3 Advanced Placement Computer Science—NSF Broadening Participation Program and the College Board, 56
        4.2.4 Carnegie Mellon University's Center on Computational Thinking, 57

5   OPEN QUESTIONS   59
    5.1 What Is the Structure of Computational Thinking?, 59
    5.2 How Can a Computational Thinker Be Recognized?, 60
    5.3 What Is the Connection Between Technology and Computational Thinking?, 61
    5.4 What Is the Best Pedagogy for Promoting Computational Thinking?, 62
    5.5 What Is the Proper Institutional Role of the Computer Science Community with Respect to Computational Thinking?, 63

6   NEXT STEPS   65

APPENDIXES

A   Workshop Agenda   69
B   Short Biographies of Committee Members, Workshop
    Participants, and Staff   74
C   Executive Summary from *Being Fluent with Information Technology* 94
D   Supplemental Bibliography   99

1

Introduction

1.1 SCOPE AND APPROACH OF THIS REPORT

This report summarizes a workshop on the nature of computational thinking held February 19-20, 2009, in Washington, D.C., under the auspices of the National Research Council's (NRC's) Committee for the Workshops on Computational Thinking. The workshop was structured to gather inputs and insights from computer scientists, information technologists, and disciplinary experts knowledgeable about how computational thinking might be relevant to their domains of expertise. It also involved a number of education researchers and cognitive scientists familiar with educational dimensions of computational thinking.

Questions posed to workshop participants included the following: What are the scope and the nature of computational thinking? How does it differ from other ways of thinking, such as mathematical thinking, quantitative reasoning, scientific thinking, and fluency with information technology? What kinds of problems require computational thinking? What are some examples? How, if at all, does computational thinking vary by discipline? What is the value of computational thinking for nonscientists? How, if at all, would widespread facility with computational thinking enhance the productivity of American workers? What affordances are provided by new technologies for computational thinking?[1] What is the role of information technology in imparting computational thinking skills?

---

[1] Loosely speaking, an affordance is the quality of an artifact that enables someone to take or perform an action. Affordances are discussed in somewhat greater detail in Section 2.5.

What parts of computational thinking can be taught without the use of computers? Without the skills of computer programming?

Although the original workshop agenda was structured around panels devoted to exploring a subset of the questions above, the discussion throughout the workshop resulted in useful insights regarding all of these questions. Accordingly, the committee organized its summary so that thoughts and insights on similar questions would be presented together, rather than being scattered throughout a summary organized in accordance with the original panel structure.

Each succeeding chapter describes some of the main themes arising from a workshop session. The themes are not conclusions or findings of the committee; they are ideas, extracted from the discussions during each session and drawn not only from the presentations of the speakers but also from the discussions among all the participants (committee, speakers, and attendees), that seem to have formed the gist of the session. In addition, to improve readability and to promote understanding, background material on some of the topics raised has been interspersed in this summary.

This report does not include all of the material that was discussed in the committee's first workshop. Specifically, in addition to discussions related to the nature of computational thinking, there were many discussions related to pedagogy and how best to expose students to the ideas of computational thinking. Because the second workshop will be devoted to that topic, the committee felt that it was better to communicate most of the first workshop's pedagogical discussions in the second workshop's report. That said, this report (of the first workshop) does foreshadow some of the themes and ideas that will be reflected in the second report. For example, the second workshop will explore possible connections between the structure and the pedagogy of computational thinking, as well as the extent to which it is reasonable to expect individuals to generalize computational thinking abilities from one problem domain to another.

In addition, the reader is cautioned that the workshop was not structured to result in a consensus regarding the scope and nature of computational thinking, and the workshop was deliberately organized to include individuals with a broad range of perspectives. For this reason and because some of the discussion amounted to brainstorming, this summary may contain internal inconsistencies that reflect the wide range of views offered by workshop participants. In keeping with its purpose of exploring the topic, this workshop summary does not contain findings or recommendations.

INTRODUCTION

1.2 MOTIVATION—WHY SHOULD ANYONE CARE ABOUT COMPUTATIONAL THINKING?

As it is usually construed, computational thinking includes a broad range of mental tools and concepts from computer science that help people solve problems, design systems, understand human behavior, and engage computers to assist in automating a wide range of intellectual processes. The elements of computational thinking are reasonably well known, given that they include the computational concepts, principles, methods, languages, models, and tools that are often found in the study of computer science. Thus, computational thinking might include reformulation of difficult problems by reduction and transformation; approximate solutions; parallel processing; type checking and model checking as generalizations of dimensional analysis; problem abstraction and decomposition; problem representation; modularization; error prevention, testing, debugging, recovery, and correction; damage containment; simulation; heuristic reasoning; planning, learning, and scheduling in the presence of uncertainty; search strategies; analysis of the computational complexity of algorithms and processes; and balancing computational costs against other design criteria. Concepts from computer science such as algorithm, process, state machine, task specification, formal correctness of solutions, machine learning, recursion, pipelining, and optimization also find broad applicability.

Computer science, of course, has no monopoly on such concepts. For example, physicists have used abstraction and modeling for centuries, logisticians and management scientists have studied scheduling extensively, and notions of tradeoff are central to the work of economists and engineers. Nevertheless, computer science provides a basis for a unified framework and language with which to discuss such notions explicitly, and these notions are the fundamental concepts of this discipline broadly construed (e.g., including information science, elements of computational science and engineering, digital media studies, and so on).

By explicitly articulating these notions, many computer scientists, and certainly the workshop attendees, believe that it is possible to describe a collection of analytic skills that everyone, not just computer scientists, can use to help solve problems, design systems, and understand human behavior. Thus, they argue, computational thinking is comparable in importance and significance to the mathematical, linguistic, and logical reasoning that society today agrees should be taught to all children.

Expanding on these ideas, workshop participants offered a number of reasons for promulgating computational thinking skills more broadly:

- *Succeeding in a technological society.* In this view, computational thinking affords individuals the ability to navigate more effectively through a society in which they frequently encounter technological devices in their personal lives (cell phones, automobiles, dishwashers, and so on). In addition, individuals have the opportunity to take advantage of technological resources (e.g., information on the Internet, social networking, online education, cloud computing). Finally, individuals competent in computational thinking are better able to understand the ways in which technology is relevant to public policy decisions. Workshop participants including Marcia Linn argued that emphasis on computational thinking in K-12 education would increase equitable access to the resources of modern society.

- *Increasing interest in the information technology professions.* It is a matter of record that enrollments in computer science university programs have dropped since the peak of the dot-com years, though in recent years, these enrollments have begun to rise again.[2] A number of workshop participants, among them Lenore Blum, argued that a broader promulgation of computational thinking in K-12 students would help to sustain the rising interest in computing as a profession.
- *Maintaining and enhancing U.S. economic competitiveness.* Some workshop participants pointed to reports that noted concerns about offshoring of U.S. jobs and the U.S. ability to remain economically competitive in a global environment.[3] In this view, a better educated workforce is an essential element of an internationally competitive workforce, and a number of workshop participants expressed the view that computational thinking is an essential component of such an education.
- *Supporting inquiry in other disciplines.* Given the increasingly prominent role that computational tools are having in other disciplines, several participants, including Edward Fox and Bill Wulf, argued that a facility with computational thinking would assist specialists in those other disciplines to more effectively adopt, use, and develop computational tools. Robert Constable pointed to some of the examples listed in Box 1.1.
- *Enabling personal empowerment.* Many workshop participants suggested that a strong motivator for an individual to learn computational thinking is to gain the ability to do things that are important to him or her. For example, Roy Pea noted that in general people want "to do something without error, do those things efficiently, and do them cost-effectively." Furthermore, people "constantly have meta-discourse around routines

---

[2] Steve Kolowich, 2009, "Computer-Science Enrollment Rises for the First Time in Six Years," *The Chronicle of Higher Education*, March 17. Available at http://chronicle.com/blogPost/Computer-Science-Enrollment/4579. Accessed December 28, 2009.

[3] See for example, National Academy of Sciences, National Academy of Engineering, and Institute of Medicine, 2007, *Rising Above the Gathering Storm: Energizing and Employing America for a Brighter Economic Future*. Washington, D.C.: The National Academies Press. Available at http://www.nap.edu/catalog.php?record_id=11463. Accessed December 28, 2009.

BOX 1.1
Computation and Computational Thinking for Creating Knowledge

1. The 1976 proof of the Four-Color Conjecture was based on an exhaustive search to evaluate an enormous number of possible cases. In 2004, the Coq theorem checker was used to confirm a variant of the original 1976 proof.
2. Computers led to the discovery that the gene regulating the size of tomatoes is similar to genes involved in cancer in mammals.[1]
3. Five new pulsars were discovered by mining 12 terabytes of data gathered from the Arecibo observatory in Puerto Rico.
4. Biologists such as Jane Hillston have used probabilistic process algebras to model the interaction of proteins within and between cells.
5. Researchers at the Joseph Bell Centre in the United Kingdom have built a system that constructs a space of hypotheses to explain the evidence in a crime scene. Such a system has been used to remind detectives of hypotheses they might otherwise have missed.
6. Predictions about climate change and global warming are enabled only through the use of computational models of planetary climate and weather. An example of an unexpected connection discovered using such models (and enormous amounts of data from automated sensors) is the influence of the surface temperature of the Indian Ocean on long-term weather patterns over the North Atlantic.
7. The Forma Urbis Romae[2] has used computers to help create new primary data from shards of the great stone map of Rome circa 210 AD by representing the shards so that they could be treated as geometric puzzle pieces that computers could attempt to assemble.
8. Computational thinking has helped to transform the Earth sciences. Without computing, geological narratives have tended to be direct, uncoupled, and linear (because such systems are easier to analyze), but such narratives underestimate the complexity of the interactions between different geological processes. Computer modeling enables Earth scientists to represent previously intractable relationships and thus helps them to develop a deeper understanding.
9. Psychologists working on the problem of how humans recognize faces have made good use of computer-based image morphing techniques. While early experiments with photos, scissors, and paste were too crude to provide the fine gradations between images needed to separate rival psychological hypotheses, Vicky Bruce and collaborators were able to show that faces are encoded in memory by abstracting them into a small collection of archetypes. Face recogni-

continued

---

[1] Anne Frary, Clint Nesbitt, Amy Frary, Silvana Grandillo, Esther van der Knaap, Bin Cong, Jiping Liu, Jaroslaw Meller, Ron Elber, Kevin B. Alpert, and Steven D. Tanksley, 2000, "T Cloning, Transgenic Expression and Function of fw2.2: A Quantitative Trait Locus Key to the Evolution of Tomato Fruit," *Science* 289(5476):85-88.

[2] Marc Levoy, 2000, "Digitizing the Forma Urbis Romae," presented at Siggraph Digital Campfire on Computers and Archeology, Snowbird, Utah, April 14.

> **BOX 1.1 Continued**
>
> tion then consists of a human matching the current image to the most similar archetype. Bruce's theory of face recognition is also formulated as a computational process, employing techniques for abstraction, representing and formulating archetypes, "nearest neighbor" matching, and so on.
>
> SOURCE: Items 1-3, 6, and 7 are adapted from Robert L. Constable, "Transforming the Academy: Knowledge Formation in the Age of Digital Information," *PhysicaPlus*, Issue 9, available at http://physicaplus.org.il/zope/home/en/1185176174/trans_academy_en. Items 4, 5, 8, and 9 are adapted from Alan Bundy, "Computational Thinking Is Pervasive," available at http://www.inf.ed.ac.uk/research/programmes/comp-think/.

and processes that help them achieve these goals." Computational thinking, Pea noted, provides people with "a way to abstract what they're already doing and talking about.... Connecting computational thinking in a personally meaningful way is at the heart of tackling the problem of how everyone can be brought into a pathway for developing and using computational thinking in their everyday lives."

2

What Is Computational Thinking?

Most of the workshop's discussions focused on exploring different aspects of what participants thought about computational thinking. The presentation of topics in this chapter is not chronological—throughout the workshop discussions, participants returned to topics and ideas mentioned earlier. Thus, the presentation below seeks to organize the discussions by theme rather than by order of presentation. Section 2.1 outlines an overview of some of the intuitive notions of computational thinking held by different workshop participants. Section 2.2 discusses computational thinking as a range of concepts, applications, tools, and skill sets. Section 2.3 looks at computational thinking linguistically (i.e., as a language) and explores the role and importance of programming as an essential aspect of computational thinking as a primary and critical mode of precise expression. Section 2.4 examines computational thinking from the perspective of automating computational abstractions. Section 2.5 looks at computational thinking as a cognitive tool set for certain kinds of intellectual endeavor. Section 2.6 explores computational thinking in contexts that do not explicitly require the use of information technology as traditionally understood. A related section (Section 2.7) explores the question of how and to what extent computers per se relate to computational thinking. Section 2.8 examines the collaborative dimensions of computational thinking. Section 2.9 presents views on what computational thinking is not.

2.1 THE LANDSCAPE OF COMPUTATIONAL THINKING

In a 2006 article, Jeannette Wing, then a professor of computer science at Carnegie Mellon University, discussed computational thinking as "a way of solving problems, designing systems, and understanding human behavior that draws on concepts fundamental to computer science."[1] Since then, Wing has assumed the position of assistant director of the National Science Foundation Computer and Information Science and Engineering Directorate. From that podium, she has promoted the idea that as computation, communications, and information become increasingly prominent throughout daily life, computational thinking becomes more useful to the economic, intellectual, and social well-being of everyone (Box 2.1).

Wing's presentation at the workshop made prominent mention of the "shotgun" approach to sequencing the human genome as a powerful example of how computational thinking might be useful outside the traditional domain of computer science. The human DNA sequence consists of 3.4 billion base pairs, and the determination of this sequence was completed in 2003, in a significantly shorter time than originally estimated, through the use of the shotgun approach. In general, the sequencing of a long DNA string can be accomplished only by dividing the sequence into a number of short fragments, each of which is sequenced and then assembled into the appropriate order.

In the shotgun approach, a long DNA sequence is randomly divided into many short fragments, each of which can be sequenced. To reassemble the fragments, investigators use overlaps between the ends of the fragments—fragments whose ends do not match cannot be connected to each other. However, the presence of a match between fragment ends does not guarantee that the two fragments in question should necessarily be joined, and additional data are needed to resolve these ambiguities. To obtain the additional data, the fragmentation process is repeated—since the division is random, it is likely that the spot where two fragments were separated in the first fragmentation will in fact be contiguous in the second fragmentation. This fact can be used to confirm or reject the match proposed from the first round. Through a series of successive rounds of fragmentation and analysis, the correct sequence can be determined. The algorithm used to analyze the data resulting from this iterative process is widely known as a shotgun algorithm.

This example manifests several aspects of computational thinking. Algorithm embodies the notion of a precisely formulated unambiguous

---

[1] Jeannette M. Wing, 2006, "Computational Thinking," *Communications of the ACM* 49(3):33-35.

> **BOX 2.1**
> **Who Is "Everyone"?**
>
> Workshop participants offered a number of definitions of "everyone." Many of the examples of computational thinking offered were directed at scientists and engineers. A few examples were connected to the needs of professionals in non-technical fields, such as archeology and law. Thus, by implication, computational thinking was thought to be relevant to a broad swath of individuals with college and postgraduate educations.
>
> Others discussed the possibility of computational thinking for K-12 students. Of course, K-12 spans a broad range. High school students take courses that address some topics that involve the same computational-thinking-related activities found in undergraduate courses. K-8 instruction is the focus of modeling and simulation environments such as Scratch and LOGO, and the NetLogo modeling and simulation environment is used primarily in middle and high schools as well as in university courses. Curricular innovations such as the honeybee example of Joshua Danish (see Figure 2.2) illustrate the possibilities.
>
> Participants did not explore the relevance of computational thinking to noncollege-educated adults in any detail. (Christopher Hoffmann did recount a tale of a group of thieves that attempted to steal a large piece of construction equipment. While the thieves prepared for most of the basic logistics surrounding the crime, they did not ultimately understand the computational-thinking-based technology at work in the system, and their efforts were ultimately thwarted. In particular, several men attempted to steal a piece of Caterpillar construction equipment by loading it on a truck to haul it away. The equipment had an active condition-based maintenance system within it broadcasting its exact location and condition as the thieves attempted to run off with the machine. They did not get far.) This topic will be explored further in the committee's second workshop.

procedure that is repetitively applied. Search, pattern matching, and iterative refinement can also be seen in the example, and the powerful idea of randomization as an asset in repeated fragmentation is a particularly important aspect of computational thinking.

Drawing on their own intuitive notions of computational thinking, workshop participants offered a number of additional examples of computational thinking in context. For instance, when a device (computer, cell phone, or printer) malfunctions, a reboot is often used to restore it to working condition. A person thinking computationally realizes that by turning it off and restarting it, she can reset the internal state of the device to a known and fresh state and allow the device's internal processes to execute from that known state. Second, information technology can help to process very large volumes of information. A person thinking computationally realizes that data-intensive problems such as sequencing DNA may be amenable to solutions based on algorithms and automation. Third, information technology can often be used to help manage complexity in understanding complicated problems. A person thinking computationally realizes that computational modeling can help address complex problems across varied disciplines such as climate change, economic policy, and educational decision making.

Responding to the workshop focus on explicating the scope and nature of computational thinking (with the implied goal of being more effective in imparting to students the essentials of computational thinking), Uri Wilensky offered a caution—that "it is not necessarily the case that the best way to enter into something is to enter it in the way that an expert already understands it." For those in attendance at the workshop, he noted that "if one is already an expert in computer science, it's easy to forget what it's like to enter into the field." He did not argue that the explication effort was wasted or inappropriate, only that as a community "we should be careful about the process of bringing a lot of people, in a widespread way, into computational thinking. We should do more than present to students expert ways of thinking computationally—attention must be paid to the developmental understanding of students." Roy Pea made a similar point when he cautioned workshop participants against focusing on the prototypes for computational thinking provided by experts in the field, because such prototypes "may lead us away from the professed goal of everyday computational thinking."

2.2 COMPUTATIONAL THINKING AS A RANGE OF CONCEPTS, APPLICATIONS, TOOLS, AND SKILL SETS

Over the course of the workshop discussion, several participants described computational thinking as a collection of mental tools and concepts from computer science that help people to solve problems, design systems, and understand human behavior. For example, Wing drew the distinction between "metal tools" and "mental tools," the former being the hardware/software applications that help solve problems and the latter being cognitive and intellectual skills that human beings can use to understand and solve problems more effectively. Participants argued that these concepts feature prominently in computer science but are not exclusive to the field.

Computational thinking was defined in a number of ways. These definitions fell into several categories and are described (in no particular order) below:

- David Moursund, along with several other workshop participants, suggested that computational thinking was closely related to, if not the same as, the original notions of procedural thinking developed by Seymour Papert in *Mindstorms*.[2] Procedural thinking includes developing, representing, testing, and debugging procedures, and an effective procedure is a detailed step-by-step set of instructions that can be mechanically interpreted and carried out by a specified agent, such as a computer or automated equipment.
- Peter Lee offered a definition of computational thinking as the study of the mechanisms of intelligence that can yield practical applications by magnifying human intelligence. Such a definition includes but is not equivalent to artificial intelligence, which in his view generally consists of efforts to mimic human mental processes. Rather, Lee argued, computational thinking is fundamentally about expanding human mental capabilities through abstract tools that help manage complexity and allow for automation of tasks. Andrew McGettrick supported this view, but went further in saying that computational "thinking" had to involve actual capability and competency with technological artifacts in addition to thought processes. Such an extended view, he noted, would require computational thinkers to constantly immerse themselves and invest in staying technologically current.
- Bill Wulf suggested that computational thinking was primarily about process. He noted that other areas of science focus on physical objects, whereas computational thinking focuses on processes and abstract phenomena that enable processes. Wulf objected to the connotations of "computational" as focusing on numbers. Speaking via videoconference, Peter Denning expressed a parallel sentiment, arguing that computer science itself is the study of information processes and that computational thinking is a subset of computer science.
- Dor Abrahamson saw computational thinking as the use of computation-related symbol systems (semiotic systems) to articulate explicit knowledge and to objectify tacit knowledge, to manifest such knowledge in concrete computational forms, and to manage the products emerging from such intellectual efforts. He further argued that a semiotic approach had embedded within it a philosophy of the relationship between understanding and personal meaning and helps guide the construction of personal meaning for these symbols.
- Gerald Sussman defined computational thinking as a way of formulating precise methods of doing things. Computational thinking is about rigorous analysis and procedures for accomplishing a defined task

---

[2] Seymour Papert, 1981, *Mindstorms: Children, Computers, and Powerful Ideas.* New York: Basic Books.

efficiently. Sussman pointed to the importance of having precise language for methods and concepts—for this reason, Sussman argued that computational thinking has an "underlying linguistic structure." For example, situations like "A happens before B" or "do this and then do that" are captured by the general idea of a partial order, and there are techniques for navigating partial orders and reasoning about them.

- Wing and Sussman suggested that computational thinking could be seen as a bridge between science and engineering—a meta-science about studying ways or methods of thinking that are applicable across the different disciplines. In this view, computational thinking is the central element of the reasoning that takes place in transitioning from the study of physical phenomena and the application of scientific observation.
- Edward Fox emphasized the notion of handling and manipulating intangible abstractions for problem-solving purposes at the core of computational thinking. Fox defined computational thinking as "what humans do as they approach the world [that is, their framing, paradigm, philosophy, or language], considering processes, manipulating digital representations (and [meta] models)," and hence all humans engage in computational thinking to some extent already in their daily lives. Brian Blake argued that computational thinking had to include representations, visualizations, modeling, or meta-modeling. Uri Wilensky pointed out the historical power of representational shifts and argued that, like other such shifts, computational representations would enable greater modeling power and wider access to scientific models. Janet Kolodner noted that computational thinking plays a role in the manipulation of software in support of problem solving. Kolodner stated that "[a piece of software can be] a tool that is being provided so that somebody can do computational thinking and can do thinking in some domain, but there's [also] some kind of computational thinking they need to be able to do in order to manipulate that tool to be able to use it for their domain."
- Robert Constable would eschew static definitions of computational thinking—rather than a finite set of skills and thought processes, computational thinking is an open-ended and growing list of concepts that reflects the dynamic nature of technology and human learning, and that combines elements of all the descriptions of computational thinking outlined above such as "automating intellectual processes" and "studying information processes," among others. What makes computational thinking especially relevant is that computers can execute our "computational thoughts" and that "computers have become partners and collaborators" in discovery. He further noted that the list of elements in the first paragraph of Section 1.2 is not merely a list of examples of computational thinking. Rather, it is a partial list of important intellectual concepts and elements that are part of the science of computing and of digital information.

> Computational thinking is careful reasoning about the methods of doing things. It's clearly related to, but not identical with, mathematical thinking. Both [computational thinking and mathematical thinking deeply] are involved with abstraction, and reasoning with simplified models.
>
> —Gerald Sussman

2.3 COMPUTATIONAL THINKING AS LANGUAGE AND THE IMPORTANCE OF PROGRAMMING

A number of workshop participants advanced the idea that computational thinking could be better understood as a fundamental intellectual skill comparable to reading, writing, speaking, and arithmetic. Functionally, these fundamental skills are all means of describing and explaining complex problems and situations to others, and computational thinking serves the same purpose. In other words, computational thinking is comparable to other basic cognitive abilities that the average person in modern society is expected to possess.

One participant quoted Niels Bohr, who said, "Science is not to tell us about the universe, but to tell us how to talk about the universe." Along these lines, computational thinking is another language (in addition to written and spoken language, science, and mathematics) that humans can use to talk about the universe and the complex processes within it.

Roy Pea argued that "as soon as we think about the origins of computational thinking and computational literacies, programming has been at the heartland of the definition and the abstractions that are created as step-by-step algorithmic procedures." Ursula Wolz supported the view that computational thinking is as essential a skill as reading, writing, and other basic language arts skills, pointing out that "programming is a language for expressing ideas. You have to learn how to read and write that language in order to be able to think in that language." Mitchel Resnick concurred, arguing that "computational thinking is more than programming, but only in the same way that language literacy is more than writing. They are both very important. Yes, it's more, but don't minimize programming just because it's more." He went on to say that programming is a particularly important form of expression, and that "programming, like writing, is a means of expression and an entry point for developing new ways of thinking." Eric Roberts also supported the idea that programming is essential to computational thinking and pointed out "a misguided assumption—that just because programming can be badly taught or that it can be difficult and deter people, it needs to be avoided entirely." (Box 2.2 describes the thoughts expressed in the 1999 report *Being Fluent with Information Technology* on the closely related question of the role of programming in imparting FITness.)

Andrea diSessa emphasized the notion of literacy as a social construction and noted that an effort to teach computational thinking (or rather, computational literacy, in diSessa's terms) to everyone is, in large part, a social problem. Moreover, it is the milieu of today's society that encourages and/or demands that citizens have this literacy. Owen Astrachan argued that "computational literacy will allow civilization to think

---

BOX 2.2
The Role of Programming in FITness

The 1999 NRC report *Being Fluent with Information Technology* addressed the role of programming in achieving fluency with information technology (what that report called FITness). The report defined programming as "the construction of a specification (sequence of instructions or program) for solving a problem by an agent other than the programmer. . . . [Programming] entails decomposing the problem into a sequence of steps and specifying them sufficiently precisely, unambiguously, and primitively that the interpreting agent, usually a computer, can effectively realize the intended solution" (p. 42).

Computer programming in a standard programming language meets this definition, of course, but programming arises in many other cases in which the agent is a human and the language is English. Giving directions to soccer players to find a particular field in a city, especially one not identifiable by numeric street/avenue coordinates, constitutes programming by this definition. A player is the agent interpreting or executing the instructions. Recipes with precise quantities of ingredients and precisely described preparation and cooking steps are programs executed by cooks. Toy manufacturers write programs, called assembly instructions, for parents to follow, and the Internal Revenue Service (IRS) writes the program that taxpayers follow for deductible IRA contributions.

Critical to the programming enterprise is specification that meets the conditions "precisely" and "primitively."

- "Precise" specifications are essential to provide assurance that the agent can determine which actions are to be performed and in what order, so that the intended result is achieved. Avoiding ambiguity is obviously crucial, but even seemingly unambiguous commands can fail. For example, "turn right" fails if the soccer players can approach the intersection from either the east or the west, and so "turn north" is preferred. Similarly, "beat" and "fold in" are not synonyms for "stir" when combining ingredients, and so successful recipes use precise terminology selected with great care. An important nontechnology advantage of programming knowledge is that the need for precision can promote precision in everyday communication.

and do things that will be new to us in the way that the modern literate society would be almost incomprehensible to preliterate cultures, but it's a different kind of literacy than what it means to be familiar. By computational literacy, I do not mean a casual familiarity with a machine that computes."

Gerald Sussman built the "computational thinking-as-basic-language" metaphor by citing the process of composing poetry as an exercise in computational thinking. A poet's task or problem is to produce a mechanism that induces an emotion in the reader of the poem. "The skillful poet takes pieces that have parts of that emotional state, puts them together

- "Primitive" specifications are essential to provide assurance that the steps to be performed are within the operational repertoire of the executing agent. The programmer may understand the task as "pi times R squared," but if the executing agent doesn't know what "squared" means or how to accomplish it, then the programmer must express the task in more primitive terms, perhaps revising it to "pi times R times R." For many taxpayers, the word "qualifying" in the IRS's instruction phrase "subtract qualifying contributions" would likely fail the test for primitiveness, because they would not readily understand what the term means.

Although programming can be as simple as giving a few commands—preheat oven to 350 degrees, combine dry ingredients, stir in eggs, press into greased loaf pan, bake for 20 minutes—most solutions require the use of conditional instructions and repetition of groups of instructions.

Conditional instructions are those that may or may not be performed, depending on the input to the program. Repeated instruction execution is a second essential programming construct, since it allows a program, for example, to process any number of data items rather than just a fixed number. In addition, FITness also requires experience with functional decomposition and functional abstraction. These are the powerful mechanisms used by programmers to solve large problems (functional decomposition) and to reuse their earlier programming efforts (functional abstraction).

Finally, the 1999 report argued that while FITness does imply a basic programming ability, that ability need not be acquired in using a conventional programming language. For example, certain spreadsheet operations and advanced HTML programming for Web pages, among others, demand an understanding of enough programming concepts that they can provide this basic programming experience. Such applications will often yield more personally relevant opportunities to learn programming than will programming in a conventional programming language.

in the right way—there are going to be bugs and there are going to have to be places where you make interfaces and all that sort of stuff—so as to make a larger structure that has that property." Sussman went on to cite an essay by Edgar Allen Poe that described the process of composing poetry as an algorithm.

Alan Kay was less enthusiastic about the "computational thinking-as-language" metaphor. Although acknowledging the utility of computational thinking as a language for describing certain aspects of the universe, Kay noted that all human beings have an innate capacity for verbal language, but that the same cannot be said for written language, science, and deductive mathematics, because these are not found in every culture or society. This point suggests that whatever computational-thinking-as-a-language might be, human beings will not learn computational thinking in the same way that they learn to speak. On the other hand, he also noted that a powerful aspect of computational thinking entails the ability to create a language well adapted to a personally relevant purpose—and indeed that this ability could be taught to students.

Edward Fox suggested that computational thinking does have a long historical tail. "Computational thinking is innate in the human species," he said, and "through telling stories our ancestors modeled and represented reality and they passed that on to other people and they enriched those models to carry out exploring, discovering, and sustaining life." Today, exploration of and discovery in digital information are central activities of human life. Computers enable modern discovery and allow humans to access and organize information in a way that has not been done before. Despite its novelty, accessing digital information is, according to Fox "still a part of this modeling and representing, something that we do uniquely and have newer ways to explain and enrich."

2.4 COMPUTATIONAL THINKING AS THE AUTOMATION OF ABSTRACTIONS

A number of workshop participants supported the claim that computational thinking focuses on the process of creating and managing abstractions, and defining relationships between layers of abstraction. Robert Constable pointed out that although physics and mathematics are also centrally concerned with abstraction, what is different in computational thinking is that the layers of abstraction are tightly connected in ways that in the natural sciences they cannot yet be connected.

In this view, computational thinking is a tool for explaining and representing complexity through automation. Although mathematics and physics are also centrally concerned with using abstraction to manage and control complexity, computational methods add another dimension to controlling complexity—that of automation. Peter Lee argued that computational thinking is about "magnifying people's intelligence through automation and problem solving, as well as managing complexity." Others pointed to the role of modeling and simulation in enabling automation of the management of complexity.

To complement this view, Andy diSessa argued that abstractions must be paired with grounding if people are to understand the significance of those abstractions. In diSessa's words, "Abstraction has to connect with their concerns, whether they are menial or whether they are grand. It has to be grounded in people's beliefs and feelings some way or other." Owen Astrachan echoed this point, saying that "without the grounded examples, we'll be talking too abstractly, which might work in a room full of abstract thinkers, but it's not going to work in rooms full of less abstract thinkers because they need to see what they are really going to do." Ken Kahn made a related argument that computational thinking provides a concretization—the creation of something concrete and tangible—of subjects that are typically dominated by abstract concepts. Kahn felt that an example of such concretization is computer games—"They are virtual, of course, but they feel very concrete. The important idea is that there is a one-to-one mapping from these concrete things to computational abstractions that are much more difficult for most people to grasp." Uri Wilensky concurred and described how students interacting with models or participatory simulations of disease spread developed with NetLogo learn to understand logistic growth of infection as an emergent pattern that results from the concrete actions of individuals.

2.5 COMPUTATIONAL THINKING AS A COGNITIVE TOOL

David Moursund saw computational thinking as how to think about tools, a view inspired by Donald Norman and David Perkins. In 1988, Norman wrote *The Design of Everyday Things*,[3] which talks about "the design of everyday objects and affordances—not just physical capabilities of the actor, but also their goals, plans, and values, and so on." An example of affordances created through technology innovation is mass communication through the creation of the printing press, radio, television, and so on. Information technology and the computer are a set of new tools with affordances of their own, and Moursund noted that realization of affordances depends on the education, training, and experience of the user as well as the design of the tool. Some tools, such as a word processor, require more formal training and skills in order to access the affordances they offer. Others, through their very design or through

---

[3] Donald Norman, 1988, *The Design of Everyday Things*. New York: Basic Books.

imitation, are simpler to manipulate and may not require formal training; examples might include telephones or video games.

In the early 1990s, David Perkins wrote about the concept of "Person Plus."[4] In the Person Plus model, three dimensions feed in to augmenting team problem solving (Figure 2.1). Moursund identified these three dimensions as "tools that expand or extend mental capabilities," such as reading comprehension or mathematical skills; "tools that extend physical capabilities," such as a car, a telescope, or a rake; and finally, "education and training" that allow one to effectively utilize tools. Moursund's final component in the model is team problem solving. He stated, "When I talk about problem solving, problem solving is always a team activity. The team might have a person on it, but the team has . . . whatever that person has learned, the culture they grew up in, the formal/informal education, and so on. So problem solving is always a team-type activity." This activity usually includes aid from physical and mental tools as well as education. Moursund believes that "computational thinking and computers fit into both categories [of tools]." Both formal and informal education can help people utilize these tools more effectively.

Moursund argued that computational thinking fuses the concepts of affordance and person with respect to information technology and computers. He spoke about the trend of increasing complexity and performance power in each generation of computers and how this trend offers new affordances and more sophisticated problem solving: "You can have a stick and you can weed your first crops with a stick. If you get a hoe, it's a much better tool. But then, with better tools, we move beyond the low-level augmentation or amplification, as it's usually called. If you get good enough tools, then you can go shooting off to the Moon and other places."

Moursund further noted, "What I see in the computer field is that there are oodles of tools where it doesn't take any formal education to learn how to use them. . . . So when we talk about computational thinking, we have oodles of tools which are just part of our everyday society and life, and which people can learn to use at a level which is personally satisfying, extends their capabilities and so on, and you don't have to go to school to learn them. That seems to me like a pretty important idea." He went on to say that in many aspects of computing and computational thinking, many people are learning on their own and learning from each other and focusing on "learning things that they want to do and need to do versus the deeper level of learning we're looking for. . . ."

Roy Pea concurred—"If you actually look at what people do when they're doing computational thinking, as an ethnographer, you see them

---

[4] David Perkins, 1992, *Smart Schools: Better Thinking and Learning for Every Child*. New York: The Free Press.

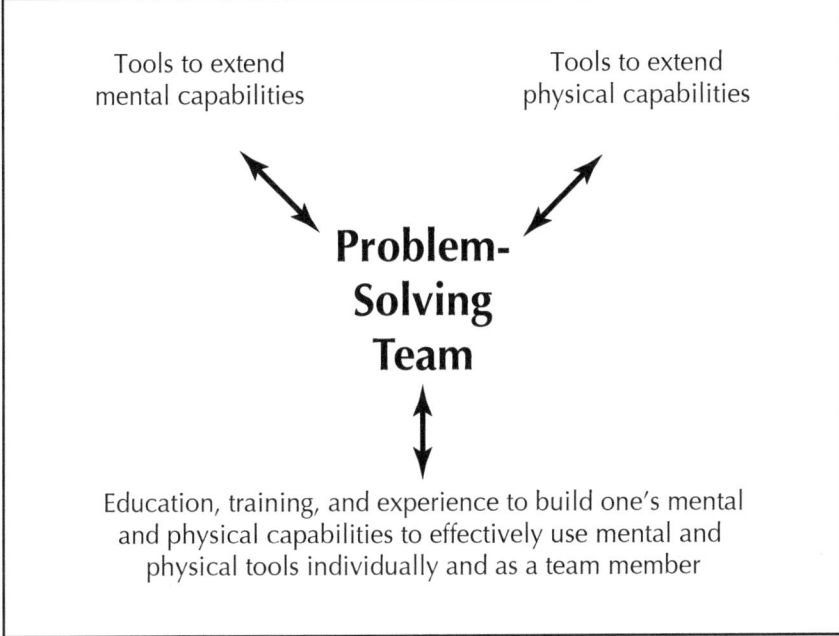

FIGURE 2.1 Perkins on problem solving. SOURCE: Adaptation by David Moursund (workshop presenter), University of Oregon, from David Perkins, 1992, *Smart Schools: Better Thinking and Learning for Every Child*, New York: The Free Press.

immersed with a whole set of tools, they're constantly thinking about the things that have particular properties, affordances—they're working with colleagues in a particular way. They're getting feedback from a whole host of resources there."

If you give everybody a calculator, math doesn't go away. Thinking and doing are needed to represent and help solve problems. If you get better tools, you can do better at it. What the computer is doing is giving you the better tools, dealing with harder problems.

—David Moursund

2.6 COMPUTATIONAL THINKING IN CONTEXTS WITHOUT PROGRAMMING A COMPUTER

Marcia Linn and several other participants discussed computational thinking as a way of approaching complex problems that permeate everyday mental activities made necessary because of the ubiquity and increasing omnipresence of computational tools throughout modern life. This way of thinking involves using methods from computer science such as debugging, search algorithms, and test cases to address everyday problems involving technological resources. Put differently, the affordances offered by modern information technology require reasoning skills such as debugging, test cases, and logical skills to solve everyday problems.

Linn pointed out that even very young children appreciate the Internet and have a sense of search, and they often take advantage of electronic devices such as cell phones and computers to access information they want. When 2-year-old Ben wanted to explain to his friend how a trapeze works, he demanded that his mother show his friend a trapeze on her cell phone. He liked the first example but wanted her to try some of the other search results. After a few minutes the battery of the phone died. Ben told his mother to turn the phone back on. He was frustrated when she tried to explain that it would take time to charge the battery. Ben already understands the power of the Internet and the nature of keyword search. Like many of us, he is confused about the limits of electrical power.

At the other end of the age spectrum, Linn used the example of retirees taking advantage of social networking opportunities to plan trips. Jack reported that he upgraded his computer to use sites like Trip Advisor to find hotels. He gained the ability to select sites that primarily serve leisure travelers rather than business travelers. He has begun to analyze the sites that support advertising—and worries that they promote the advertised products. He prefers sites where the qualifications of the reviewers are available. He has developed a theory about who posts on these sites and has started to realize that many people really do not articulate their criteria. Jack is using his debugging skills.

Joshua Danish presented an example of young students engaging in computational thinking concepts without using computers in a project on honeybees—specifically to understand and represent the process honeybees use to collect nectar for honey. This process involves a beehive sending out scouts to locate flowers with nectar; these scouts then return to the hive and do a "dance" to communicate the location of the nectar to the other bees. Other bees then return to the specified location to harvest the nectar.

Danish said, "Here [in Figure 2.2] is a student's representation in four panels of that process, and it's actually quite nice. Now, there are limitations to that. But we're starting to see some of the skills and the resources—and this is a 7-year-old's drawing—and when they're actually

FIGURE 2.2 A dance of the bees. An elementary student's four-panel drawing modeling a complex sequence—the process bees use to communicate the location of a viable source of nectar. SOURCE: Joshua Danish, Indiana University.

starting to be quite capable of reducing and extracting that process and describing it for us."

In the first phase of activity, students engaged in an individualized "creation of representations"—that is, each student drew his or her own detailed picture of a single bee (subject to certain minimum requirements, such as having three body sections and including the proper names of key parts of the bee) and also a series of four panels (Figure 2.2) depicting the process bees use to find nectar, collect nectar, and then communicate the location of the nectar to the hive.

Next, the children were asked to engage in "participatory modeling" of the bees collecting nectar, an idea first introduced as such by Uri Wilensky and Mitchel Resnick.[5] Children produced a skit in which they represented flowers and bees and proceeded to demonstrate how a bee goes about collecting nectar. Danish argued that this activity allows students "to leverage their ability and make sense of talk and gesture and body position as a way of refining their model and understanding the parts of it that they may not have formal language for yet."

For example, the students were able to refine their models through repetition, "debug" their models through collaboration, and explore sequencing. Danish described a boy representing a bee that had just checked for nectar—his peers did not actually see him using a proboscis,

---

[5] Uri Wilensky and Mitchel Resnick, 1999, "Thinking in Levels: A Dynamic Systems Perspective to Making Sense of the World," *Journal of Science Education and Technology* 8(1):3-19.

and so "they were challenging his model, saying, we don't see the part of the bee that's important for that part of the process." The teacher is also able to introduce the concepts of sequencing and algorithms by engaging in a dialog with the student:

> T: All right, well, there isn't any nectar at that flower. So if you were a bee, would you stay at the flower?
> S: No.
> T: What would you do?
> S: I would go back, and not do a dance because I don't know where to find nectar.

According to Danish, this exchange illustrates how the student is engaging "in a context where he's able to talk about the sort of if-then choices of the algorithm that the bees follow as they go back collecting nectar. And that can then be phrased in a way that's incredibly relevant to him."

In the third phase, students engaged in participatory simulation in which they had to instruct other children to carry out the search for nectar as the bees would. As they tried to act the instructions provided by the scout bees, the children engaged in a real-time debugging process by updating their instructions as they went along. This phase forces the students into "thinking about the implications of their modeling choices. As these students are running around and not quite finding the nectar, it's easy for this boy to say, 'It's by the red rake.' So there's some online monitoring of whether or not his instructions or his program were successful. But then there's also some retroactive consideration, some nice reflection on whether that model did the job. So the student's then able to say, 'I should have said by the handle of the rake.'"

Only in the fourth phase did students encounter any actual computer technology—with the help of an instructor, students modeled the process and predicted outcomes using a program called BeeSign, developed to provide a simulation environment for students to model bee searches.

A second example of computational thinking in a non-IT context was provided by Ursula Wolz, who reported on an effort to teach computational thinking skills to middle school students through the journalistic use of interactive media. She described the project as focusing on a "non-didactic collaborative model of problem solving." Journalism provides an attractive context for students who do not consider themselves technically inclined.

Wolz argued that journalism mirrors many of the processes involved in working with computers, especially programming. "In journalism, one must pitch a story, research it, interview, collect data, shoot video, write, edit, send it to the editor, re-write, add sidebars, resubmit, fact check, debug the story, and loop until the editor signs off on it. If one assumes the computer acts as an editor, then one can take note of a very familiar series of activities involved in computational thinking." The students had news teams, supervised by a teacher and guidance counselors, that worked to produce an online magazine. The students researched, interviewed, and wrote stories, and they created video and animation in Scratch. They also successfully used the computing environment used to support the course to collaborate, write, edit, and publish multimedia stories as part of the journalism process.

A third example of computational thinking without computers was provided by Tim Bell, who described the Computer Science Unplugged Project.[6] His talk included a couple of illustrations:

- *User interfaces.* Students examine the interface provided in a digital watch. In many digital watches, a button is included that turns the watch face from a clock to a stop watch, and another button that starts and stops the stop watch. According to Bell, "Suddenly the kids realize that this is a very simple interface, which they probably didn't even think was an interface, on their wrist." This realization empowers them to recognize interfaces in other objects and apply learned concepts when interacting with those objects. User interfaces are an important element of computational thinking because they create a well-defined decoupling between the parts of the system that interact directly with users and the rest of the system. User interfaces thus afford a structured and systematized method of entering input into a program that in turn affects its behavior. User interfaces also afford users such methods for seeing program outputs.
- *Routing.* Each student wears a T-shirt of a different color (Figure 2.3). Corresponding to each color are two pieces of fruit, and every student except one starts with two pieces of fruit. One student starts with only one piece of fruit of the appropriate color. The goal is to have both pieces of fruit end up in the hands of the child with the corresponding color shirt; that is, "the oranges go to the girl with the orange T-shirt and the green apples go to the girl with the green T-shirt," and so on. The constraint on any method of passing fruit is that each student can only pass something to someone who has an empty hand, and he or she can only pass something to a neighbor. This puzzle is similar to the kinds of problems that a computer scientist might face, and students can experiment with different routing topologies. Routing is an important element

---

[6] Tim Bell, Ian H. Witten, and Mike Fellows, 2006, *Computer Science Unplugged: An Enrichment and Extension Programme for Primary Aged-Children.* Canterbury, New Zealand: Computer Science Unplugged.

FIGURE 2.3 Routing fruit (packets). SOURCE: Tim Bell, University of Canterbury-Christchurch, New Zealand.

of computational thinking because it encapsulates the idea of how information can be passed in different paths through intermediate nodes to a specified final destination.

A third example of computational thinking without the use of technology per se was provided in a personal anecdote from Owen Astrachan. He described different solutions to a word puzzle in which the problem solver must change a given five-letter word (e.g., "white") to another five-letter word (e.g., "house") by making only a single letter change at each step, subject to the constraint that each intermediate word must also be a real dictionary word. Astrachan's solution was based on making a graph and doing a breadth-first search through that graph. His solution required 16 steps. His brother, an English major, solved the problem in 15 steps, apparently without using computational thinking. Astrachan then asked why, and saw that his brother's solution was based on the fact that his brother's dictionary had more words in it—"sough" was in his brother's dictionary but not in his. With the addition of that word to Astrachan's solution, he was able to solve the problem in 14 steps. Astrachan said that this story illustrates computational thinking in action and computational thinking in context, and helps to demonstrate "what's going on with people around us who don't think computationally."

Allan Collins argued that one key feature of computational thinking is representational competence, which he described as the effective application of computational means of representation of knowledge. The illustration Collins offered was a low-tech experiment in developing representational competence in fourth graders who were asked to "find representations for the heights" of various fast-growing plants. The children were broken up into several groups, and each group of kids would try to come up with its own representations. While there were a number of ideas considered, the class eventually decided to "use a bar graph with small ranges of plants . . . like from 10 inches to 12 inches, and they would have a bar for each two inches."[7]

And then in terms of the survey results that we got, the majority . . . said the most important thing they learned was programming and video editing. And half said that their best work was in programming. And unlike some of the kids that Alan [Kay] and Roy [Pea] were talking about, these are working-class children who would not necessarily have access to this level of computing unless it was through a program like this.

—Ursula Wolz

As computation came in, it started producing all sorts of new forms of representation, both structural forms and process forms, particularly the dynamic process forms . . . things like production rules and frames and semantic networks and the constraint-satisfaction systems were all new ways to think about representing knowledge. . . . And so my claim is that one of the things that we should be concerned about is how to get this kind of *representational competence*. We need to start thinking more seriously about how we can convey some of that power.

—Allan Collins

---

[7] Collins also cited the work of Rich Lehrer and Leona Schauble and their work with really young kids and getting them to think about how to represent distributions and statistical reasoning. See Richard Lehrer and Leona Schauble, 2004, "Modeling Natural Variation Through Distribution," *American Educational Research Journal* 41(3):635-679.

2.7 THE ROLE OF COMPUTERS AND TECHNOLOGY

An obvious question arises in the consideration of computational thinking. How and to what extent do computers per se relate to computational thinking?

A first point is that the term "computer" can refer to a mechanical or an electronic computer, or to a human computer (indeed, the first connotation of the word "computer" was that of a human who performed mathematical computations). So a computer is an essential aspect of computational thinking to the extent that it is an agent that can deterministically interpret a set of instructions in an unambiguous manner.

A more common interpretation of the question relates to whether or not a competent computational thinker is necessarily facile with the use of modern information technology to solve problems and to do other useful things. Workshop participants observed that information technology has advanced dramatically throughout its history, and rapid change is likely to characterize future information technology. Moreover, computers and computation will become increasingly important to society and across a number of disciplines. As one participant put it, "I think we are here today to think about what everybody should know" in the face of such rapid change.

Many participants argued that the ability to develop facility with new technologies is a part of computational thinking. Computational thinking in this view involves finding the right technology for a problem and applying the technology to resolve the problem. This might require learning how to use the appropriate technology, debugging the solution, and communicating the outcome. For example, to represent a complex phenomenon such as an ecosystem, the moves in a chess game, or the trajectory of a baseball, the computational thinker might explore alternative technologies, select a candidate, and test its effectiveness. This skill is essential in undergraduate programs, useful in everyday life, and growing in importance in precollege courses. In this view computers and other computational devices enable computational thinking.

One participant argued that what makes computational thinking especially relevant is that computers, whether mechanical or human, are the agents for executing "computational thoughts," and computers have become partners and collaborators in discovery. Further, unlike household appliances or an automobile, computers are relevant to a vast number of different applications, such as searching for information, developing a budget, tracking individuals, composing music, and so on. While not disagreeing with this sentiment, others at the workshop argued strongly that because computers are not restricted to mechanical computers but instead can refer to human agents, computational thinking becomes relevant to individuals outside the context of mechanical computers—and thus to a much larger cross section of society.

2.8 A COLLABORATIVE DIMENSION TO COMPUTATIONAL THINKING

Modern information technology is at least as much about dispersed, real-time communication as it is about automation. Edward Fox noted that "what we see happening a lot today, especially with the Web and multimedia and other things, is that the [computational thinking] reflection takes place with the help of other people, too. We can share videos and we see what other people did and we comment on those. We have Web 2.0 and so forth, where these become social processes, and debugging becomes part of our society, as well as of solving our problems."

Building on this notion, a number of participants suggested that computational thinking could be regarded as a group phenomenon as well as an individual one. That is, groups, too, can engage in computational thinking to develop representations, debug processes, and so on, resulting in a collective process of discovery that is richer than that of any single individual. Ursula Wolz argued this point when she said that "one of the things that annoys me is when we talk about some of the great discoveries that happened by an individual—they never happened by an individual. There is a huge body of literature emerging, for example, in terms of what Leonardo did and who was around, and the same thing about Newton. . . . We have to keep reminding ourselves that it isn't about ownership. It's about the community and the culture that's around you that allows you to have the ideas."

Allan Collins related collaboration to the notion of computational thinking as a fundamental skill analogous to reading and writing literacy. He pointed out that developing reading and writing literacy is not simply a matter of technical skills, but also arguably entails a social community. In Collins' words, "We learn from the company we keep. . . . People will learn to read and write if the people they admire and care about, the communities they belong to, are readers and writers." Thus, he argued, achieving a comparable literacy with respect to computational thinking will require the fostering and development of communities that value computational thinking—some of which exist today, though not in large numbers and not widely accessible.

Kevin Ashley introduced an example of collaborative computational thinking from the legal field. Over time, the legal community performs testing and adaptation of laws in response to changing social contexts. He pointed out, "Often the hypotheticals are informed by changes in societal values over a period of time; this is dynamic. The old law has to be reevaluated, reinterpreted in the context of the changing social values. The hypotheticals—the specific examples that they try out to see how that would be dealt with under the proposed rule and whether that is a good outcome or not in light of those values—are the dynamic engine for adapting the rules and interpretations to the new circumstances."

> In some sense, I think the message that Roy [Pea] is delivering, that I, [and] Mitchel [Resnick] are delivering, is that we need to start thinking about how to create communities of people who care about computational thinking and who are doing it.
>
> —Allan Collins

2.9 WHAT COMPUTATIONAL THINKING IS NOT

Several participants suggested that it might be easier to articulate what computational thinking is not. For example, Robert Constable argued that computer literacy—traditionally seen as the ability to use specific programs or features of given computer systems such as Word or Excel—does not demonstrate the ability to engage in computational thinking. (By contrast, he noted that one can know a great deal about computational thinking and computing concepts without knowing much about computers beyond how to get on the Internet and use an Internet browser.)

Along with a number of other workshop participants, Gerald Sussman argued that computational thinking was also not equivalent to computer science. Although computational thinking and computer science share some elements, he said that "computational thinking is a certain part of computer science. Mathematicians talk about *mathematical thinking*. Statisticians talk about *statistical thinking*. I think that computer scientists should talk about *computational thinking*." To illustrate, he said that "scientific thinking is about apples and oranges and how they may be different or the same. Mathematical thinking is about spheres and where they have areas and volume and the fact that they may involve a particularly high number of dimensions. Computational thinking is about how a group of people can cut and share an apple so that each person feels he or she got a fair share of the apple."

> I know some people have been saying things like, computational thinking is a new way to define computer science. Computational thinking is a part of computer science, but is not the whole story.
>
> —Peter Denning

> **BOX 2.3**
> **Great Principles of Computing**
>
> In 2003, Peter Denning initiated the "Great Principles of Computing" project, whose purpose is to express the activities of computer science in a framework that is similar to that which guides scientists in other domains in expressing what it is that they do. During the workshop, Denning said that he and his colleagues are very interested in "the fundamentals of the field," the things that are "timeless and . . . also illustrate the depth and richness of the discourse that we have built up in computing over the years." Denning's Great Principles of Computing break down into seven categories: computation, communication, coordination, recollection, automation, evaluation, and design.
>
> Denning's framework portrays computer science as a combination of engineering, mathematics, and science. During the workshop, Denning argued that a legitimate science is based on "knowledge, experimental methods, reproducibility, surprising predictions complemented by performing art, and studies of natural objects," and hence that computer science should be included under this rubric. He acknowledged that "there has always been controversy about whether computer science studies natural objects," but expressed the belief that "other fields are now accepting that information processes are part of the basic aspects of nature." He further suggested that this acceptance stems from evolving the definition of computer science away from a strict focus on computing machines—"We are coming to see computation as the principle and the computer as the tool. Instead of the computer being at the center of what we study, computation is at the center of what we study. That shift in perspective allows us to see computation in nature."

Other participants felt that computational thinking was the outcome of a natural evolution in our understanding of computer science. For example, Peter Denning suggested that computational thinking is not the same as previous conceptions of computer science, but rather another instantiation of the discipline (Box 2.3).

Larry Snyder noted that computational thinking was not the same as fluency with information technology (FIT)[8] (Appendix C), although they do share many commonalities (Box 2.4). For example, many of the features often ascribed to computational thinking are also part of a fluency curriculum that include both concepts and capabilities. These concepts include algorithmic thinking, managing complexity, debugging, thinking technologically, universality, and so on. Indeed, he suggested that the

---

[8] NRC, 1999, *Being Fluent with Information Technology*, Washington, D.C.: The National Academies Press. Available at http://www.nap.edu/catalog.php?record_id=6482. Accessed December 28, 2009.

> **BOX 2.4**
> **On the Relationship Between Computational Thinking and Fluency with Information Technology**
>
> A person who is highly capable of computational thinking—a computational thinker—is one who has adopted the thinking habits and reasoning methods of computer scientists. A person who is fluent with information technology is one who has adopted a specific menu of facts, concepts, and thinking habits of computer scientists. In this sense, computational thinking is broader than fluency.
>
> On the other hand, because the fluency menu includes algorithmic thinking and a variety of intellectual capabilities such as sustained logical reasoning and debugging, there is tremendous overlap between computational thinking and fluency. When discussing specific topics (as opposed to levels of understanding of a topic), there are strong similarities between the intellectual approaches embedded in each. Both emphasize abstraction, algorithmic thinking, problem solving, logical reasoning, levels of abstraction, universality, debugging, technological point of view, representations, and so on. Such strong similarities are why the knowledge needed and acquirable as "basic computational thinking" would likely approximate what is known by a person fluent with information technology.
>
> The primary difference between computational thinking and fluency is in focus. In one view of this difference, the primary emphasis of pedagogical efforts in fluency is quite clearly on the general population, and there is relatively little emphasis on its applicability to advanced topics of study. By contrast, computational thinking is believed to be valuable across the board, both for the everyday citizen and for the advanced professional. Indeed, many of the examples of computational thinking that advocates invoke are derived from the application of computational thinking in service of these advanced professionals in a variety of problem domains. Another view of the difference between computational thinking and fluency sees computational thinking as emphasizing conceptual understanding and fluency as emphasizing applications across a broad range of topics and problem domains.
>
> Another difference is that whereas fluency prescribes a variety of skills that enable a citizen to use certain computer-enabled devices daily, computational thinking is not concerned at all with such skills—such skills are assumed. Fluency does include a set of 10 concepts about computing and 10 intellectual capabilities that include many of the habits of mind often captured in descriptions of computational thinking, but an important purpose of including these concepts and capabilities is to support lifelong learning about computing.
>
> Computational thinking and fluency should not be placed in opposition to each other, though they are definitely not the same thing. Computational thinking is a grand vision in which people acquire the thinking habits of computer scientists commensurate with their levels of education; fluency, though not originally formulated this way, can be seen as a practical implementation of computational thinking for all citizens. This difference reflects the differing origins of the studies involved—the *Being Fluent* report (National Research Council, *Being Fluent with Information Technology*, National Academy Press, Washington D.C., 1999) and its characterization of fluency with information technology emerged from responding to a request for recommendations on what the public should know about information technology, while the present report on computational thinking emerged from a vision of how beneficial wider use of thinking like a computer scientist would be.

primary difference was the fact that FITness includes a skills component, which is designed to enable individuals to use common current applications. By contrast, computational thinking tends to put less emphasis on specific technical skills in favor of broad problem-solving abilities.

Snyder also called attention to a philosophical evolution regarding computing-related teaching. The FITness report was published in 1999,[9] when it was controversial to teach conceptual material regarding information technology to nonmajors. Snyder argued that today, such teaching is routine, at least in 4-year university programs. He thus proposed the following sketch for this philosophical evolution:

- The general public is uninformed about and indifferent to information technology.
- The general public recognizes the need for computer literacy—how to use a computer—a necessary skill as computers begin to penetrate into everyday life.
- The general public begins to see the limitations of skills-only training, which leads to a desire for FITness—fluency with information technology—that exposes citizens to the essential concepts and capabilities of information technology. The skills of FITness are gradually de-emphasized as the citizenry learns to pick up without formal instruction the skills needed to use computer applications.
- The general public is increasingly exposed to and literate with the skills of how to use information technology, thus eliminating the need for much formal instruction in skills. Computational thinking, which to first order comprises FITness without the skills component, becomes the emerging focus of formal education. Computational thinking then expands the array of concepts and capabilities beyond those included in the original 1999 formulation of FITness.

Others saw computational thinking as a way of thinking that is qualitatively distinct from fluency and emerging across a broad array of disciplines. The ubiquitous nature of computational tools impacts all aspects of modern life and requires people to adopt new modes of thinking to use these tools effectively. These modes of thinking are emerging not just in computer science but in every field.

---

[9] NRC, 1999, *Being Fluent with Information Technology*, Washington, D.C.: The National Academies Press. Available at http://www.nap.edu/catalog.php?record_id=6482. Accessed December 28, 2009.

I would like to propose that this is actually a three-dimensional problem. We have aspects of computational thinking or computing, we have the other disciplines that we are talking about connecting with, and we have pedagogy, the different levels and so forth. We are trying to populate a three-dimensional matrix with the best situations in each of these different settings and figure out which ones are the ones that work.

—Edward Fox

3

Looking Outward

3.1 THE RELATIONSHIP OF COMPUTATIONAL THINKING TO MATHEMATICS AND ENGINEERING

For some, computational thinking is careful reasoning about the methods of doing things that complements and combines mathematical and engineering thinking. The special relationship of computational thinking to mathematics is historical, but looking toward the future, computational thinking will be critical in the social and life sciences as well. Computational thinking currently plays an important role in psychology, linguistics, graphics, and economics and is playing an increasing role in complex engineering efforts such as nanoscience and health. Computational thinking will apply much more broadly than most of the other scientific modes of thought. The conceptual space to which computational thinking applies is much broader than most people imagine, and many of the advances are independent of the usual constraints on natural science.

3.1.1 Mathematical Thinking

Computational thinking is closely related to, but not identical with, mathematical thinking. Both are deeply involved with abstraction and reasoning with recognized simplified models. Gerald Sussman argued that computational thinking and mathematics both have an "underlying linguistic structure ... [that is] language for precise descriptions and about how to do things and language describing the structure of things ... such languages are essential to clear thinking. But mathematical thinking is more about abstract structure than abstract methodology." Jeannette Wing also added the qualifier that while similar to mathematical thinking in many respects, computational thinking does have to consider the physical constraints of the underlying computer (whether machine or human).

Paulo Blikstein highlighted that since both mathematics and computational thinking are tools for representation, there may be an opportunity to use computational thinking to represent complex processes and relationships in a more comprehensible manner than mathematics. One example he provided came from his observations of how engineering courses were taught. He immediately noticed that within a common engineering course, mathematical equations appear "approximately one every 2 minutes." Blikstein added that often these equations are around 10 variables long, and insufficient time is allocated to actually explain the equations. He thinks that "this speaks to the failure of one particular way to think about knowledge and one way to represent knowledge, which is representing knowledge as differential equations and mathematical forms in general. . . . Computational representations might offer a lot of advantages over mathematical representations that we might be able to explore."

Sussman gave an example of teaching students how to analyze electrical circuits. He noted that the typical pedagogical approach for this problem is to teach the node method—which in practice many students find difficult to implement in any practical way in solving problems in circuit theory. However, presenting students with a well-written computer program designed to solve such problems as an expert would enable them to internalize the program themselves and execute it much as that expert would.

3.1.2 Engineering

Several workshop participants recognized an overlap between engineering and computational thinking. Even if it is not formally accepted in the engineering community, engineering schools are "doing a lot of computational thinking," said Blikstein. Wing argued that both computational thinkers and engineers think about design, constraints, safety, performance, and efficiency. Design issues considered include "simplicity, elegance, usability, modifiability, maintainability, and cost. Wing said that "computational thinking is guided by particular concerns/constraints such as speed, space, and power [and computational thinking is] more like physics and engineering in this respect. . . . [It is] these kinds of concerns that determine how good an abstraction is. When we are defining abstractions, of course, it is very similar to engineering thinking."

At the same time, computational thinking is unlike engineering. As Wing pointed out, "In software we can basically do anything; we can actually build virtual worlds that are unconstrained by physical reality." Sussman argued that as contrasted to engineering involving physical objects, "computational thinking is engineering where we are not given a hard time by the fact that the physical world produces tolerances, that there is error in the construction of parts. As a consequence, instead of being limited as we are in mechanical or electrical engineering by tolerances and that sort of thing, we are only limited by the things we can think about, by the complexity that we can control in our minds." In other words, computational thinking invents the abstractions that it manipulates.

Peter Lee noted that several of the 14 engineering grand challenges for the 21st century identified by the National Academy of Engineering had a strong information technology/computer science/computational thinking flavor to them. These included reverse engineering of the human brain; advancing personalized learning; securing cyberspace; enhancing virtual reality; advancing health informatics; and engineering the tools of scientific discovery.[1]

One important aspect of the computational thinking–engineering connection is managing complexity. Engineered systems are becoming more and more complex. But Bill Wulf noted that software engineering was arguably the first field to face challenges related to complexity, and the need to manage complexity is important in computational thinking. As noted in the *Being Fluent with Information Technology* report,[2] managing complexity entails tradeoffs. For example, one solution to a problem may involve complex design but entail straightforward implementation, whereas another may involve a simple design but a costly implementation. A solution will often result in components of a system interacting in complex, unexpected ways, and the resources available to implement a solution may be inadequate. Managing such dimensions of a problem's solution is an exercise in managing complexity.

So I like to think about computational thinking as complementing and combining mathematical and engineering thinking. For instance, we clearly draw on mathematics as our foundations. We also draw on engineering, since our systems actually operate in the real world.

—Jeanette Wing

---

[1] See National Academy of Engineering, "Grand Challenges for Engineering." Available at http://www.engineeringchallenges.org/. Accessed December 28, 2009.

[2] NRC, 1999, *Being Fluent with Information Technology*. Washington, D.C.: The National Academies Press. Available at http://www.nap.edu/catalog.php?record_id=6482. Accessed December 28, 2009.

3.2 DISCIPLINARY APPLICATIONS OF COMPUTATIONAL THINKING

Workshop participants shared their experiences in applying computational thinking in different fields to illustrate how computational thinking might be relevant. Brian Blake described the exchange as "trying to understand how computational thinking, as it is embedded in computer science or computational fields, is used in noncomputational fields to see how what we know in the computational field can be used in other fields." The hope was expressed that by describing some of these different applications, it would be possible to identify concepts of computational thinking through its application in one discipline that could be utilized to benefit another discipline and indeed to better define and describe computational thinking.

- *Medicine and health care.* Peter Lee described how sequencing techniques commonly employed in computational thinking can help to improve the chance of success in matching organ donors. On a small scale, the task of cross-matching multiple donors and patients is a relatively simple computational thinking exercise. At the large scale at which the medical profession would need to perform these matches to improve donation matching across the nation, this type of matching poses a significant intellectual challenge for computational thinking practitioners. Ian Foster noted that the medical profession is currently trying to cope with enormous amounts of crucial but confidential data. This information must be easily accessed and transferred among medical professionals to improve care but protected from access and misuse by those outside the medical profession. Foster argued that with the advent of *health care informatics*, "health care is arguably no longer a medical problem, but a computing problem."
- *Archeology.* Edward Fox works with archeologists attempting to look at trends across different excavation sites. He said that the archeologists he collaborates with have come to realize that "if you are going to study archaeological trends across different areas, and the commerce that takes place between sites, then you have to merge the data and you have to use common terminology." For example, archeology often depends on archived data, where differences in recording protocols, terms, measurement units, and languages make accessibility a challenge.[3] Moreover, archeological researchers need to organize large amounts of qualitative data so that they can be retrieved computationally. Computational thinking approaches to information retrieval, data fusion, and information

---

[3] Dean R. Snow, Mark Gahegan, C. Lee Giles, Kenneth G. Hirth, George R. Milner, Prasenjit Mitra, and James Z. Wang, 2009, "Cybertools and Archeology," *Science* 311 (5763):958-959.

integration are especially useful in this area, since there is a need "to classify and search for numerical, textual, and visual data simultaneously" and a need for "an e-science that marries the interconnectedness of digital research tools with the introspection enabled by traditional recordkeeping."[4]

- *Traffic engineering.* Modern-day traffic lights are usually run by computer systems that alternate traffic signals based on algorithms and embedded sensors and networks. The most effective traffic algorithms are built using data collected on traffic patterns and other relevant variables in order to optimize flow. The processes by which these algorithms are developed and tested involve computational thinking. The methods skilled drivers may use to navigate them also reflect computational thinking. Christopher Hoffmann noted the example of the veteran bus driver: "The bus driver should know that if he steps on it [the gas pedal] too fast, he gets stuck at the next traffic light anyway."

- *Cancer research.* Peter Lee noted that agent-based modeling simulations have helped researchers understand that a "tumor is not really a simple group of cells that have their own agenda. They tend to live in an environment where the cells nearby sort of form a nurturing matrix for them and respond to various requests from the tumor for additional blood vessels, for example, or nutrients or whatever. This is something that invalidates a lot of the existing medical science and puts it more into a systems-thinking context, something that I think we [computational thinking scholars] can contribute to."

- *Public policy.* An increasingly technology-based society creates the need for techno-savvy policy makers. For example, important issues related to information technology regarding privacy, copyright, and spectrum allocation are prominent on the public policy agenda, issues for which an understanding of computational thinking is very helpful. Bob Sproull illustrated the point by suggesting that a legislator might need an understanding of computational thinking in order to be a smart customer of a complicated IT system for the Social Security Administration or the Internal Revenue Service.

- *Music.* Peter Lee described a summer program where young students attempt to write computer programs that allow computers to compose original music. The program challenged students to write a "computer program that could compose or a machine that could take as input some description of Bach and then produce beautiful music." The process of building such systems makes use of computational thinking in three ways. First, it requires that a programmer analyze and decompose

---

[4] Dean R. Snow, Mark Gahegan, C. Lee Giles, Kenneth G. Hirth, George R. Milner, Prasenjit Mitra, and James Z. Wang, 2009, "Cybertools and Archeology," *Science* 311 (5763):958-959.

musical qualities into abstract computational thinking concepts. Second, the program must construct algorithms and programming language that access and demonstrate the aforementioned musical qualities artificially. Finally, by observing this process of decomposition and composition, one can learn more about human intelligence and problem-solving processes.

- *Law.* Kevin Ashley discussed four ways computational thinking applications advance the legal practice: logic debugging, testing, modeling, and information retrieval.

> —Debugging through the reduction or elimination of "syntactic ambiguity" or "logical ambiguity" is almost always present in any kind of legal drafting. Whether in statutes, contracts, or insurance policies, unintentional ambiguities in legal language are common and must be debugged. Ashley commented that this process involves "getting the logic right, in a manner that's kind of similar to what computer programmers have to do in getting the logic right in a line of code."
>
> —The development of good test cases reflects an important similarity between computational and legal thinking—both test propositions (or statements) against test cases. "Test cases are important in debugging in programming as well [as in law]—real and hypothetical counterexamples, exceptions, things like that." Ashley pointed out that they can help a legal professional anticipate how successful an argument is likely to be by simulating the application across various test cases.
>
> —Modeling complex legal processes and flows can help legal professionals to understand "the flow of control through a statute, for the process of statutory interpretation, for predicting outcomes, for structured arguments."
>
> —Information retrieval techniques are needed for legal information systems that can represent the justifications and context in a reasonable way. Ashley pointed to the role of precedent, or relevant preceding judgments in similar cases, in legal arguments. Computational thinking can help lawyers to develop good targeted searches based on complex criteria.

Ashley also expressed a caution that computational thinking might lead to over-mechanization of complex processes. "Legal problem solving is highly context-dependent in ways that may not be anticipated. As a law professor, I have to be very cautious about recommending computational thinking to law students, because it might lead them to focus more on a mechanical application of a predefined method rather than on the context and the opportunities in the actual problem to be solved. I have an obligation not to mislead. We don't want mechanical jurisprudence here. I think this caution probably applies in a lot of other areas as well."

- Al Aho referred to Christos Papadimitriou's talk "The Algorithmic Lens: How the Computational Perspective Is Transforming the Sciences"[5] as an exemplar of a compelling story about the power of computational thinking. Briefly, Papadimitriou presented a number of vignettes from mathematics, physics, biology, economics, and social science to show the unifying power of computation across these disciplines:

—In mathematics, the classic P versus NP from theoretical computer science was named as one of the seven Clay Institute Millennium Problems,[6] which pose the deepest, most fundamental, and consequential open problems in the field.

—In physics, quantum computation provides a method for exploring and testing the limits of quantum mechanics. Further, how phase transitions can be explained in statistical mechanics turns out to have deep similarities to the way that certain randomized algorithms converge exponentially faster when their parameters are in the right range (analogous to the temperature/pressure of a physical system being at the critical point of a transition).

—In biology, understanding the mechanism of evolution can be productively approached as an algorithmic problem. Using optimization theory and search to compare simulated annealing and genetic algorithms as ways to sketch landscapes of fitness functions, it can be shown that genetic algorithms tend to find plateaus in the landscape, while simulated annealing finds peaks. Plateaus in the landscape have the characteristic of being relatively broad and thus relatively stable for many genetic combinations. Since simulated annealing is analogous to asexual reproduction and genetic algorithms to sexual reproduction, this approach suggests that rather than maximization of fitness, sexual reproduction favors adequacy, or more specifically the ability of a genetic variant to function adequately in the presence of a wide variety of genetic partners.

—In economics and social science, the Internet—an IT artifact constructed but never designed—must be studied using the methods of natural science (e.g., observation and experimentation) and in the context of the complex social system it enables and serves. It is thus an ideal test bed for sociological analysis and experimentation.

---

[5] Christos H. Papadimitriou, 2009, "The Algorithmic Lens: How the Computational Perspective Is Transforming the Sciences." Available at http://www.scivee.tv/node/10204. Accessed December 28, 2009.

[6] For more information see Clay Mathematice Institute, "P vs NP Problem," available at http://www.claymath.org/millennium/P_vs_NP/, accessed December 28, 2009.

Complementing these perspectives, a number of participants including Bob Constable noted the importance of acknowledging a two-way street for connecting computational thinking to various disciplines. That is, it is not only that other disciplines can benefit from the use of computational thinking in their respective domains—it is also the case that the computer science and information science disciplines from which much of computational thinking is derived benefit from understanding the basis of knowledge creation in those other disciplines. Indeed, those other disciplines provide a context for computational thinking that often leads to new discoveries in computer science and information science themselves.

3.3 COMPUTATIONAL THINKING ACROSS DIFFERENT DISCIPLINES

The subsections below are organized around different elements of computational thinking that have widespread application in multiple disciplines.

3.3.1 Problem Solving/Debugging

Several speakers emphasized debugging of systems as an important application of computational thinking. In the real world, people often encounter systems with which they are unfamiliar and whose internal workings they do not understand. Robert Sproull pointed out that when humans encounter such systems, they often attempt to establish "a known state" of the system or a state of functionality that they find familiar or intuitive. This behavior is an aspect of modeling the unfamiliar system in their minds, despite the fact they may not necessarily know what sorts of algorithms are inside.

To develop these models and identify known states, an individual (or group) builds on previous experience and encounters with similar systems to generate hypotheses about how it works, about what its parts are, and so on. Debugging can then be done in a variety of ways. One can, for instance, adjust parameter settings to attempt to debug a system.

You know something about debugging that you have learned from dealing with even more complex things. It carries over as a set of techniques, not just because it was your computer program that you were debugging rather than a dishwasher.

—Robert Sproull

3.3.2 Testing

In the sense used here, testing refers to empirical activities that provide information about whether and how a software artifact or system performs in accordance with its performance requirements. For all but the simplest artifacts, it is not feasible to test a system for all possible inputs, and so good testing procedures call for test suites, which generally involve typical cases, boundary cases, and potential failure conditions. For a listing of different kinds of testing appropriate at different stages in an artifact's lifetime, see http://www.softwareqatest.com/qatfaq1.html#FAQ1_10.

Children encounter many opportunities to engage in testing. One participant used the example of a robotics competition to explain how students engage in testing. Robots are designed to perform specific tasks, and designers must test their performance. Even if there is no computing inside the robot, Sproull noted, "even if it's just a joystick driving a servo, you have to figure out how to test it."

3.3.3 Data Mining and Information Retrieval

Popular culture often describes the modern society in a constant state of information overload. Computational thinking provides intellectual tools to help manage information. For example, a computational thinker will understand a variety of ways for retrieving information. Edward Fox commented that computational thinking can help people who are accessing lots of information from a number of data sources to represent it in some common way and to find ways to communicate their results.

3.3.4 Concurrency and Parallelism

Ursula Wolz described a number of ways to expose students to the computational concepts of concurrency and parallelism. For example, a college junior majoring in music took Wolz's introductory course to fulfill a quantitative reasoning requirement. Wolz's course uses Scratch, an application for manipulating animated characters, and according to Wolz, "the first thing he ran up against was the problem of synchronicity between music and animation." With a few simple examples (offered by a more advanced student), the music major said, "I get it." Wolz offered a second example of a sixth-grade student who worked on animation of comparable sophistication using PowerPoint. In both cases, Wolz suggested that their successes in understanding concurrency and parallelism were due not so much to the Scratch graphical environment as to the metaphors that help convey understanding of the underlying concept.

Mitchel Resnick described a simple programming exercise in which the user choreographs a dance for an animated cat. The "code" is structured to represent interlocking blocks. Each block contains a specific set of instructions. For example, if a user wants the sound of drums followed by the cat moving forward, then she would take the drum block, interlock the forward step block, and indicate the number of steps forward. In this particular activity, users can see for themselves how programming, sequencing, algorithmic thinking, and parallel thinking play out. In Resnick's words, "Parallelism comes very naturally. If I say, while it's doing that, I also want to keep changing the color . . . [then] I just have another stack that says I want to forever change the color. So it takes some of the computational ideas of sequencing, and parallelism, and tries to make it very easy to put together and explore these ideas."

3.3.5 Modeling

To illustrate computational thinking, Mitchel Resnick used a personal example based on his standing Monday tennis match. Every week, he and his partner Ken record who wins how many games in each set, the number of games, and the number of sets. At the end of the year, they have a record of the number of games and the number of sets that each player won. One year, they noticed that Ken had won 54 percent of the games but 71 percent of the sets, and they asked, "What's the explanation behind that?"

Coming from very different disciplines—Ken in biology and Mitchel in computer science/education—each player conceptualized and approached this question very differently. Ken's explanation the next week was based on handwritten calculations involving expansions of a binomial expression. Mitchel's explanation was based on a simulation of matches and replicating the data using children's instructional software called Scratch. The program was developed to determine "randomly for each game that Ken has a 55 percent chance of winning [and] I have a 45 percent chance of winning." As the simulation was repeatedly run, the total wins-to-losses ratio closely reflected the real-life outcome.

More generally, modeling is a means by which one represents a system or a process in order to learn more about it and manage complexity. One participant mentioned the power of computational thinking to improve the effective development of complex models through knowledge of scale. Peter Lee argued that a computational thinker "understands the consequences of scale" and can thus "think very big and very small and understand the tipping points at each point." As more data are gathered, the more sophisticated the model one can build to describe a system. If there is sufficient fidelity in a model, one can perform necessary testing within the model itself. Computers and computation can dramatically increase the amount of data represented in these models and thus a model's fidelity. An example using computational thinking to model plane crash testing is shown in Figure 3.1.

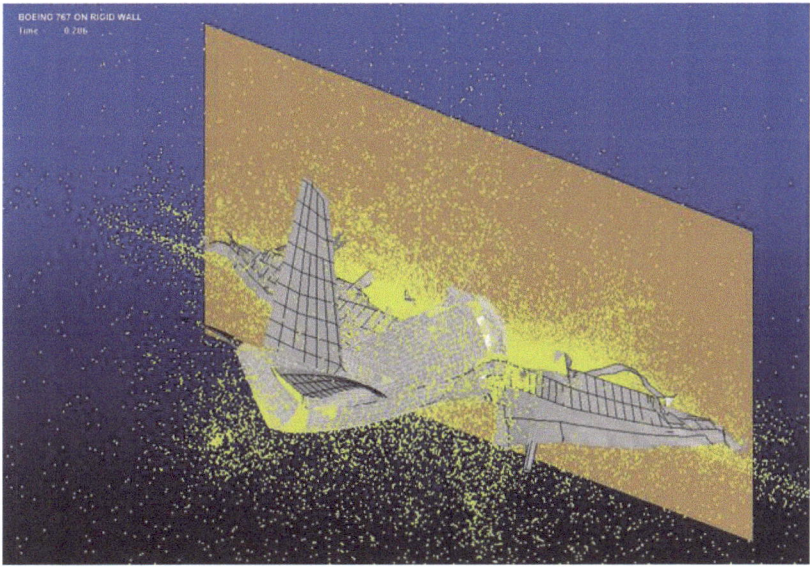

FIGURE 3.1 Modeling of an airplane crash. (Top) Image of a crash test measuring the force of impact on an actual F-4 Phantom airplane; image courtesy of Sandia National Laboratories. (Bottom) Image of a computational model of the force of impact on an aircraft; image courtesy of Christopher Hoffmann, Purdue University.

Paulo Blikstein complemented this perspective when he described bifocal modeling, wherein the physical and the virtual were blended in models, sometimes by using the physical world as inputs to a model, by calibrating a model, or by comparing the output of model mechanisms to sensor data. He argued that such blending was becoming more common in the practice of science and was also a powerful means of engaging students.

Yasmin Kafai noted an example of the importance of understanding models and their limitations: "Government authorities often use models to make predictions, but people often don't understand how these models were made, what the parameters are, or what kind of assumptions are underlying them . . . here we have a really great example . . . [in talking] about computational thinking for everyone and kind of as a goal for citizenship [in] that citizens need to also understand how decisions are being made and what some of the pitfalls in the models will be." Wilensky added that computational thinking involves more than using models, experimenting with models, or even constructing them; it also involves creating a culture of model critique.

4

Relationship to Past and Ongoing Efforts

4.1 PREVIOUS WORK

A number of past activities and reports have argued for introducing computational thinking to populations broader than undergraduates and graduate students matriculating in computer science or information technology. In addition, several reports have sought to identify what computer scientists believe is the intellectual core of their discipline.

4.1.1 LOGO

In the 1960s, Seymour Papert introduced the notion of a computer-based microworld that could serve as an environment in which a child could learn "to manipulate, to extend, to apply to projects, thereby gaining a greater and more articulate mastery of the world, a sense of the power of applied knowledge and a self-confidently realistic image of himself as an intellectual agent." He argued that computation could have "a profound impact by concretizing and elucidating many previously subtle concepts in psychology, linguistics, biology, and the foundations of logic and mathematics" by giving a child the ability "to articulate the working of his own mind and particularly the interaction between himself and reality in the course of learning and thinking."[1]

---

[1] Seymour Papert, 1975, "Teaching Children Thinking," *Journal of Structural Language* 4:219-29.

As an example, Papert offered mathematics. He argued that many children never see the point of the formal use of language, which is what much of mathematics teaches. They also rarely, if ever, have the experience of designing a formalism of their own adapted to a particular personally meaningful task. But anyone who programs a computer does these things routinely. Through the construction of specialized formal microworlds, the LOGO environment is intended to provide appropriate terminology and concepts that facilitate the formal use of language and the child-driven extension of that language in useful ways. By programming the computer to do interesting things, Papert argued, children can become highly sophisticated and articulate in the art of developing models and developing formal systems.

A number of workshop participants, Uri Wilenksy among them, also pointed out that although many of the intellectual ideas introduced by the LOGO movement are quite similar to those underlying the advocacy of computational thinking, there are many significant differences in the larger environment in which these activities were and are embedded. Forty years ago, when LOGO was first introduced, computational infrastructure was expensive, and access to networking and personal computing was non-existent for all practical purposes. Today, computational devices are everywhere, and access to networking and personal computing are quite commonplace. Moreover, the idea that computational technology could have a deep impact on everyday life for most citizens—outlandish then—is now easily accepted, and thus the ubiquitous presence of computational devices in our lives is an important motivator for systems of formal education to provide individuals with appropriate intellectual tools for managing and using such devices effectively.

4.1.2 Fluency with Information Technology (FIT)

The 1999 report *Being Fluent with Information Technology*, also known as the FITness report or the fluency report, was an effort by the Computer Science and Telecommunications Board of the National Research Council to articulate what everyone should know about information technology.[2]

In formulating the relevant knowledge base, this effort identified three equally important categories of knowledge: cognitive/intellectual capabilities, computational concepts, and IT skills. *Capabilities* focus on logical reasoning and problem solving such as debugging. *Concepts* rep-

---

[2] NRC, 1999, *Being Fluent with Information Technology*. Washington, D.C.: National Academy Press. Available at http://www.nap.edu/catalog.php?record_id=6482. Accessed December 28, 2009.

resent the fundamental ideas that underlie technology, such as programming and algorithms. Finally, *skills* are the actual knowledge required when using information technology, such as creating a Word document or sending an e-mail.

The attempt to define "everyone" was more problematic—although the members of the responsible committee likely believed, as individuals, that all K-12 students should be exposed to the elements of IT fluency, and indeed should become fluent with information technology, none of the committee members had any particular standing to make such an assertion, and in the end the committee limited the scope of its recommendations to all graduates of 4-year colleges and universities.

The executive summary of *Being Fluent with Information Technology* is reprinted as Appendix C.

I think the goals of the fluency report were [answering the question] what should everybody know to be a more effective user of technology? And I think that computational thinking focuses more on [the] intellectual activities that apply to all of the sciences and engineering that we talked about, and [also] all those other areas that could benefit from computation. So it seems to me that they're slightly different objectives. I don't see them as in conflict. . . . They overlap a lot because they do speak to a similar set of phenomena.

—Lawrence Snyder

4.1.3 Computing the Future

In 1992, the National Research Council issued the report *Computing the Future*,[3] which was (among other things) the first Academy effort to articulate the nature of computer science and engineering as an intellectual discipline. That report noted the following (pp. 19-24):

> Intellectually, the "science" in "computer science and engineering" connotes understanding of computing activities, through mathematical and engineering models and based on theory and abstraction. The term "engineering" in "computer science and engineering" refers to the prac-

---

[3] NRC, 1992, *Computing the Future: A Broader Agenda for Computer Science and Engineering*. Washington, D.C.: National Academy Press. Available at http://www.nap.edu/catalog.php?record_id=1982. Accessed December 28, 2009.

tical application, based on abstraction and design, of the scientific principles and methodologies to the development and maintenance of computer systems—be they composed of hardware, software, or both. [The notion of CS&E as a discipline based on theory, abstraction, and design is described in Peter Denning, Douglas E. Comer, David Gries, Michael C. Mulder, Allen Tucker, Joe Turner, and Paul R. Young, 1989, "Computing as a Discipline," *Communications of the ACM*, 32(1):9-23, January.] Thus both science and engineering characterize the approach of CS&E professionals to their object of study.

What is the object of study? For the physicist, the object of study may be an atom or a star. For the biologist, it may be a cell or a plant. But computer scientists and engineers focus on information, on the ways of representing and processing information, and on the machines and systems that perform these tasks.

The key intellectual themes in CS&E are algorithmic thinking, the representation of information, and computer programs. An algorithm is an unambiguous sequence of steps for processing information, and computer scientists and engineers tend to believe in an algorithmic approach to solving problems. In the words of Donald Knuth, one of the leaders of CS&E:

> CS&E is a field that attracts a different kind of thinker. I believe that one who is a natural computer scientist thinks algorithmically. Such people are especially good at dealing with situations where different rules apply in different cases; they are individuals who can rapidly change levels of abstraction, simultaneously seeing things "in the large" and "in the small." [Personal communication to the NRC Committee to Assess the Scope and Direction of Computer Science and Technology, Donald Knuth, March 10, 1992, letter.]

The second key theme is the selection of appropriate representations of information; indeed, designing data structures is often the first step in designing an algorithm. Much as with physics, where picking the right frame of reference and right coordinate system is critical to a simple solution, picking one data structure or another can make a problem easy or hard, its solution slow or fast.

The issues are twofold: (1) how should the abstraction be represented, and (2) how should the representation be properly structured to allow efficient access for common operations? A classic example is the problem of representing parts, suppliers, and customers. Each of these entities is represented by its attributes (e.g., a customer has a name, an address, a billing number, and so on). Each supplier has a price list, and each customer has a set of outstanding orders to each supplier. Thus there are five record types: parts, suppliers, customers, price, and orders. The problem is to organize the data so that it is easy to answer questions like: Which supplier has the lowest price on part P?, or, Who is the largest customer of supplier S? By clustering related data together, and by constructing auxiliary indices on the data, it becomes possible to answer such questions quickly without having to search the entire database.

The two examples below also illustrate the importance of proper representation of information:

- A "white pages" telephone directory is arranged by name: knowing the name, it is possible to look up a telephone number. But a "criss-cross" directory that is arranged by number is necessary when one needs to identify the caller associated with a given number. Each directory contains the same information, but the different structuring of the information makes each directory useful in its own way.
- A circle can be represented by an equation or by a set of points. A circle to be drawn on a display screen may be more conveniently represented as a set of points, whereas an equation is a better representation if a problem calls for determining if a given point lies inside or outside the circle.

A computer program expresses algorithms and structures information using a programming language. Such languages provide a way to represent an algorithm precisely enough that a "high-level" description (i.e., one that is easily understood by humans) can be mechanically translated ("compiled") into a "low-level" version that the computer can carry out ("execute"); the execution of a program by a computer is what allows the algorithm to come alive, instructing the computer to perform the tasks the person has requested. Computer programs are thus the essential link between intellectual constructs such as algorithms and information representations and the computers that enable the information revolution.

Computer programs enable the computer scientist and engineer to feel the excitement of seeing something spring to life from the "mind's eye" and of creating information artifacts that have considerable practical utility for people in all walks of life. Fred Brooks has captured the excitement of programming:

> The programmer, like the poet, works only slightly removed from pure thought-stuff. He builds castles in the air, creating by the exertion of the imagination.... Yet the program construct, unlike the poet's words, is real in the sense that it moves and works, producing visible outputs separate from the construct itself.... The magic of myth and legend has come true in our time. One types the correct incantation on a keyboard, and a display screen comes to life, showing things that never were, nor could be. [Frederick Brooks, 1975, *The Mythical Man-Month,* Reading, Mass.: Addison-Wesley.]

Programmers are in equal portions playwright and puppeteer, working as a novelist would if he could make his characters come to life simply by touching the keys of his typewriter. As Ivan Sutherland, the father of computer graphics, has said,

Through computer displays I have landed an airplane on the deck of a moving carrier, observed a nuclear particle hit a potential well, flown in a rocket at nearly the speed of light, and watched a computer reveal its innermost workings. [Ivan Sutherland, 1970, "Computer Displays," *Scientific American* 222(6):56-81.]

Programming is an enormously challenging intellectual activity. Apart from deciding on appropriate algorithms and representations of information, perhaps the most fundamental issue in developing computer programs arises from the fact that the computer (unlike other similar devices such as non-programmable calculators) has the ability to take different courses of action based on the outcome of various decisions. Here are three examples of decisions that programmers convey to a computer:

- Find a particular name in a list and dial the telephone number associated with it.
- If this point lies within this circle then color it black; otherwise color it white.
- While the input data are greater than zero, display them on the screen.

When a program does not involve such decisions, the exact sequence of steps (i.e., the "execution path") is known in advance. But in a program that involves many such decisions, the sequence of steps cannot be known in advance. Thus the programmer must anticipate all possible execution paths. The problem is that the number of possible paths grows very rapidly with the number of decisions: a program with only 10 "yes" or "no" decisions can have over 1000 possible paths, and one with 20 such decisions can have over 1 million. . . .

The themes of algorithms, programs, and information representation also provide material for intellectual study in and of themselves, often with important practical results. The study of algorithms within CS&E is as challenging as any area of mathematics; it has practical importance as well, since improperly chosen algorithms may solve problems in a highly inefficient manner, and problems can have intrinsic limits on how many steps are needed to solve them. The study of programs is a broad area, ranging from the highly formal study of mathematically proving programs correct to very practical considerations regarding tools with which to specify, write, debug, maintain, and modify very large software systems (otherwise called software engineering). Information representation is the central theme underlying the study of data structures (how information can best be represented for computer processing) and much of human-computer interaction (how information can best be represented to maximize its utility for human beings).

4.1.4 Reflections on the Field

The 2004 NRC report *Computer Science: Reflections on the Field, Reflections from the Field* included an essay by Gerald Sussman entitled "The Legacy of Computer Science."[4] Quoting from that essay (pp. 181-183):

> Computer Science is not a science, and its ultimate significance has little to do with computers. The computer revolution is a revolution in the way we think and in the way we express what we think. The essence of this change is the emergence of what might best be called procedural epistemology—the study of the structure of knowledge from an imperative point of view, as opposed to the more declarative point of view taken by classical mathematical subjects. Traditional mathematics provides a framework for dealing precisely with notions of "what is." Computation provides a framework for dealing precisely with notions of "how to." [Harold Abelson, Gerald Jay Sussman, with Julie Sussman, 1985, *Structure and Interpretation of Computer Programs* (1st edition), Cambridge, Mass., MIT Press.]
>
> Computation provides us with new tools to express ourselves. This has already had an impact on the way we teach other engineering subjects. For example, one often hears a student or teacher complain that the student knows the "theory" of the material but cannot effectively solve problems. We should not be surprised: the student has no formal way to learn technique. We expect the student to learn to solve problems by an inefficient process: the student watches the teacher solve a few problems, hoping to abstract the general procedures from the teacher's behavior with particular examples. The student is never given any instructions on how to abstract from examples, nor is the student given any language for expressing what has been learned. It is hard to learn what one cannot express.
>
> In particular, in an introductory subject on electrical circuits we show students the mathematical descriptions of the behaviors of idealized circuit elements such as resistors, capacitors, inductors, diodes, and transistors. We also show them the formulation of Kirchoff's laws, which describe the behaviors of interconnections. From these facts it is possible, in principle, to deduce the behavior of an interconnected combination of components. However, it is not easy to teach the techniques of circuit analysis. The problem is that for most interesting circuits there are many equations and the equations are quite complicated. So it takes organiza-

---

[4] NRC, 2004, "The Legacy of Computer Science," pp. 181-183 in *Computer Science: Reflections on the Field, Reflections from the Field*. Washington, D.C.: The National Academies Press. Available at http://www.nap.edu/catalog.php?record_id=11106. Accessed December 28, 2009.

tional skills and judgment to effectively formulate the useful equations and to deduce the interesting behaviors from those equations.

Traditionally, we try to communicate these skills by carefully solving selected problems on a blackboard, explaining our reasoning and organization. We hope that the students can learn by emulation, from our examples. However, the process of induction of a general plan from specific examples does not work very well, so it takes many examples and much hard work on the part of the faculty and students to transfer the skills.

However, if I can assume that my students are literate in a computer programming language, then I can use programs to communicate ideas about how to solve problems: I can write programs that describe the general technique of solving a class of problems and give that program to the students to read. Such a program is precise and unambiguous—it can be executed by a dumb computer! In a nicely designed computer language a well-written program can be read by students, who will then have a precise description of the general method to guide their understanding. With a readable program and a few well-chosen examples it is much easier to learn the skills. Such intellectual skills are very hard to transfer without the medium of computer programming. Indeed, "a computer language is not just a way of getting a computer to perform operations but rather it is a novel formal medium for expressing ideas about methodology. Thus programs must be written for people to read, and only incidentally for machines to execute." [Harold Abelson, Gerald Jay Sussman, with Julie Sussman, 1985, *Structure and Interpretation of Computer Programs* (1st edition), Cambridge, Mass., MIT Press.]

I have used computational descriptions to communicate methodological ideas in teaching subjects in electrical circuits and in signals and systems. Jack Wisdom and I have written a book and are teaching a class that uses computational techniques to communicate a deeper understanding of classical mechanics. Our class is targeted for advanced undergraduates and graduate students in physics and engineering. In our class computational algorithms are used to express the methods used in the analysis of dynamical phenomena. Expressing the methods in a computer language forces them to be unambiguous and computationally effective. Students are expected to read our programs and to extend them and to write new ones. The task of formulating a method as a computer-executable program and debugging that program is a powerful exercise in the learning process. Also, once formalized procedurally, a mathematical idea becomes a tool that can be used directly to compute results.

4.1.5 Engineering in K-12 Education

The National Academy of Engineering (NAE) and its Committee on K-12 Engineering Education issued a report arguing that an engineering component has been largely missing in recent attempts to improve science, technology, engineering, and mathematics (STEM) education.[5] The NAE committee found this fact particularly troubling in light of its view that ". . . K-12 engineering education may improve student learning and achievement in science and mathematics; increase awareness of engineering and the work of engineers; boost youth interest in pursuing engineering as a career; and increase the technological literacy of all students." That committee also hypothesized that the "future of K-12 engineering education" will depend on whether engineering becomes a more interconnected component of STEM education or remains a separate subject.

The report noted that unlike mathematics and science education in the K-12 years, engineering education does not have much in the way of teaching standards, testing and assessment, or teacher professional development. More broadly, the committee held that there is "no widely accepted vision of what K-12 engineering education should include or accomplish. This lack of consensus reflects the ad hoc development of educational materials in engineering and that no major effort has been made to define the content of K-12 engineering in a rigorous way. . . . These shortcomings may be the result, at least in part, of the absence of a clear description of which engineering knowledge, skills, and habits of mind are most important, how they relate to and build on one another, and how and when (i.e., at what age) they should be introduced to students."

To improve engineering education, the report noted the importance of emphasizing engineering design, incorporating important and developmentally appropriate mathematics, science, and technology knowledge skills (among which were certain "computational methods"), and promoting engineering habits of mind (i.e., the values, attitudes, and thinking skills associated with engineering). Such considerations are relevant to the discussion of this workshop report because of the strong connections between many such engineering habits of mind and computational thinking. The report also called for research on various dimensions of engineering education (including its connection to other STEM fields) and for the initiation of a national dialogue on preparing K-12 educators to address the special challenges of engineering education at the K-12 level.

4.1.6 Technically Speaking

In 2002, the National Academy of Engineering and the NRC issued the report *Technically Speaking: Why All Americans Need to Know More*

---

[5] National Academy of Engineering and National Research Council, 2009, *Engineering in K-12 Education: Understanding the Status and Improving the Prospects*. Washington, D.C.: The National Academies Press. Available at http://www.nap.edu/catalog.php?record_id=12635. Accessed December 28, 2009.

About Technology[6] and its companion website.[7] This report advanced a view of technological literacy that encompasses three interdependent dimensions—knowledge, ways of thinking and acting, and capabilities with the goal of providing people "with tools to participate intelligently and thoughtfully in the world around them":

- Knowledge for technological literacy consists of a recognition of the pervasiveness of technology in everyday life, an understanding of basic engineering concepts, an understanding of the limitations of the engineering process, a knowledge of ways technology has shaped human history and vice versa, a recognition that technology reflect the values and culture of society, a recognition of technology risk, both anticipated and unanticipated, and an awareness that technology development involves cost/benefit tradeoffs.
- Ways of thinking and acting for technological literacy include questioning oneself and others regarding benefits and risks associated with technology, actively seeking information about new technologies, and actively taking part in decisions about the development and use of technology.
- Some of the basic capabilities the report points to as characteristic in a technically literate person include certain hands-on technical skills like word processing or navigating online, an ability to identify and fix simple technical malfunctions, and an ability to think about benefits and risk in basic mathematical terms.

These three dimensions have approximate mappings to the tripartite framework of FITness (foundational concepts, intellectual capabilities, and contemporary skills), as discussed in Box 2.2.

4.2 SOME DRIVERS OF CHANGE

Workshop participants described a number of ongoing efforts to revise and reform computing-related education. Implicit in these efforts is a presumption that they will all have to address computational thinking in some form, but for the most part, their efforts had not converged on a common definition of the term.

---

[6] National Academy of Engineering and National Research Council, 2002, *Technically Speaking: Why All Americans Need to Know More About Technology.* Washington, D.C.: National Academy Press. Available at http://www.nap.edu/catalog.php?record_id=10250. Accessed December 28, 2009.

[7] For the companion website, see National Academy of Engineering, "Technically Speaking," available at http://www.nae.edu/techlit, accessed December 28, 2009.

4.2.1 The National Science Foundation CPATH Program

In 2008, the Computer and Information Science and Engineering (CISE) Directorate of the National Science Foundation launched a program entitled "CISE Pathways to Revitalized Undergraduate Computing Education" (CPATH).[8] This program emphasizes the development of student competencies in computing concepts, methods, technologies, and tools (which collectively constitute what the program calls computational thinking) in approaches that promise to revitalize undergraduate education.

Founded on the importance of preparing a globally competitive U.S. workforce that is able to apply computational thinking to a broad range of societal challenges and opportunities, the program seeks to contribute to the development of a globally competitive U.S. workforce with computational thinking competencies essential to U.S. leadership in the global innovation enterprise; to increase the number of students developing computational thinking competencies by infusing opportunities for learning computational thinking into undergraduate education in the core computing fields—computer and information science and engineering—and in other fields of study; and to demonstrate transformative computational-thinking-focused undergraduate education models that are replicable across a variety of institutions.

Although aimed primarily at revitalizing undergraduate education, the program also encourages the exploration of new models that extend from institutions of higher education into the K-12 environment. Activities that engage K-12 teachers and students to facilitate the seamless transition of secondary students into undergraduate programs focused on computational thinking are particularly encouraged.

4.2.2 The Computing Research Association Education Committee

Andrew Bernat described for workshop participants some of the present-day efforts (2009) of the Computing Research Association (CRA) Education Committee.[9] Stressing the importance of revitalizing computing education and noting the centrality of computers and computing to

---

[8] For more information, see NSF Directorate for Computer and Information Science and Engineering (CISE), "CISE Pathways to Revitalized Undergraduate Computing Education (CPATH) FAQ Site," available at http://www.nsf.gov/cise/funding/cpath_faq.jsp, accessed December 28, 2009, and CISE Pathways to Revitalized Undergraduate Computing Education (CPATH) Program Summary," available at http://www.nsf.gov/funding/pgm_summ.jsp?pims_id=500025&org=CNS&from=home, accessed December 28, 2009.

[9] For more information, visit the Computing Research Association at http://www.cra.org/, accessed December 28, 2009.

a number of fields—art, music, history, and archeology, as well as the traditional sciences and engineering—Bernat said that these efforts focus on "the computing education that a researcher in any discipline needs to know and think about and understand. It is not intended to be the undergraduate curriculum that someone going on to do computer science should be exposed to or should learn. It's about researchers in any discipline. What are the core things about computing that everyone needs to understand?" Bernat further emphasized that in contrast to groups such as the ACM that are focusing on education in computer science, the CRA intends to focus its efforts on computing skill, knowledge, and impact outside the computer science discipline.

4.2.3 Advanced Placement Computer Science— NSF Broadening Participation Program and the College Board

Jan Cuny described for workshop participants the NSF/College Board collaboration to redesign and revitalize the high school Advanced Placement (AP) Computer Science (CS) curriculum.[10,11] According to Cuny, the current CS AP course is inaccessible to students and fails to introduce the fundamental concepts of computational thinking. Cuny expressed the hope that a new "gold-standard" AP course that addresses these concepts will revive the flagging interest of high school students in computer science, information technology, and mathematics and will provide a foundation for future study in computing.

She pointed out that developing the curriculum for this new course is not the most challenging aspect. The hardest part is to gain entry into "resource-strapped schools." Nevertheless, Cuny hopes that this new gold-standard CS AP course can be introduced into 10,000 schools (with a complement of 10,000 teachers trained to teach the course) by 2014. She was not unmindful of the challenges, pointing out that most of these teachers are not computer scientists themselves. "Most of them are from math or from physics or from chemistry and they know how to program . . . but they don't know about computability. They don't know about algorithm design. There's a whole lot of stuff that they don't know. So it's not just in-service preparation, meaning bring them in for a week. It's really significant training that we have to provide. And we have to figure out how to make that palatable for them."

---

[10] The College Board, "National Science Foundation Awards $1.8 Million to College Board to Redesign AP Science Courses." Available at http://www.collegeboard.com/press/releases/51572.html. Accessed December 28, 2009.

[11] NSF Directorate for Computer and Information Science and Engineering (CISE), "Broadening Participation in Computing (BPC)." Available at http://www.nsf.gov/funding/pgm_summ.jsp?pims_id=13510&org=CNS&from=home. Accessed December 28, 2009.

Finally, Cuny raised the related point that it is important to distinguish between ideas and concepts that can be tested on a standardized exam and what it means to assess whether students can think computationally. In the absence of a consensus on the scope and nature of computational thinking, she noted that it would be very difficult to develop an appropriate assessment tool for the latter.

4.2.4 Carnegie Mellon University's Center on Computational Thinking

Carnegie Mellon University's Center for Computational Thinking is the home to a number of projects that focus on using computational thinking to tackle broad social and interdisciplinary issues. According to Peter Lee, these projects—known as PROBlem-oriented Explorations, or PROBEs in the local vernacular—cover a wide range of ongoing research projects, all of which are designed to demonstrate the critical importance of computational thinking. These projects typically engage the sciences, the arts, and literature.[12]

- During the workshop, Lee pointed to the Optimal Kidney Exchange PROBE, which uses novel algorithm design and database networking to identify optimal kidney matches between donors based on a complex set of criteria. Traditionally, kidney matching is done manually by medical experts based on blood type, organ size, patient condition, and so on. The manual methods used by most physicians also tend to look at a small number of donors and patients—paired donations (involving two donors coordinating their donations) are the most common. By using larger numbers of coordinated donors (8 or 10 or 12 donors at a time), the number of organs made available that can match the needs of individual recipients can be vastly increased. However, the complexity of coordinating larger numbers of donors is quite daunting, unless efficient computational algorithms can be used to perform the search. The result is that medical experts can match kidneys among a much larger number of patients and donors in a number of kidney exchange programs more rapidly. More effective kidney exchanges can improve the quality of life for those on dialysis currently awaiting kidneys, save millions in medical costs for dialysis treatments, and save thousands of lives.

- Discussed on the center's website, the Performer PROBE is an interactive music system for live performance that is capable of composing

---

[12] See the Center for Computational Thinking, Carnegie Mellon University, "PROBEs," available at http://www.cs.cmu.edu/~CompThink/probes.html, accessed December 28, 2009.

and accompanying live music in different genres, such as classical, rock, and Latin.[13] Unlike systems that merely accompany human-performed music and require a strict adherence to beat and score, Performer will be able to interact with other human musicians, change tempo, and even change styles in a manner that is similar to how a human would behave in such a situation. Performer employs modeling, sequencing, synchronicity, algorithms, human-computer interaction theory, sensors, and data management theory to dissect nuances of music composition and music performance.

- The center's website also discusses the PROBE on Understanding and Harnessing Ensemble Behavior,[14] which uses the "programming" metaphor to understand how the behavior of components aggregate to produce behavior in complex systems, whether natural or man-made. Although the complex system is "just" the aggregation of its constituent components, the capabilities of the system far exceed the aggregate of the capabilities of those components. Using a specially developed programming language called Meld, the project demonstrates abstraction, programming, logic, ensemble engineering, self-organization, robotics, and programming in the context of understanding emergent behavior. Meld is designed to streamline the process of programming for ensemble systems, and it works by propagating the commands that input through every node in the system, thus saving the programmer the time needed to propagate the command herself.

---

[13] See the Center for Computational Thinking, Carnegie Mellon University, "PROBEs," available at http://www.cs.cmu.edu/~CompThink/probes.html, accessed December 28, 2009.

[14] See the Center for Computational Thinking, Carnegie Mellon University, "PROBEs," available at http://www.cs.cmu.edu/~CompThink/probes.html, accessed December 28, 2009.

5

Open Questions

As noted in the preface, NRC workshops are not designed to produce consensus. However, although there was little general agreement among workshop participants about the essential nature of computational thinking, a number of questions did emerge that are worthy of attention in the future.

5.1 WHAT IS THE STRUCTURE OF COMPUTATIONAL THINKING?

Throughout the course of the workshop, participants expressed a host of different views about the scope and nature of computational thinking. But even though workshop participants generally did not explicitly disagree with views of computational thinking that were not identical to their own, almost every participant held his or her own perspective on computational thinking that placed greater emphasis on particular aspects or characteristics of importance to that individual. (These different perspectives are described in Chapter 2.)

Given this divergence in individual emphases, one possibility concerning structure is that computational thinking is simply the union of these different views—a laundry list of different characteristics. On the other hand, such a perspective would be both incoherent and deeply unsatisfying to most workshop participants, and there was general agreement that a more coherent perspective is needed. Further thought about many questions emerging from the workshop is thus warranted; these questions include:

- What is the core of computational thinking?
- What are the elements of computational thinking?
- What is the sequence or trajectory of development of computational thinking?
- Does computational thinking vary by discipline?

Some of the logical subquestions that follow include:

— What are the logical relationships between the various elements of computational thinking?
— What elements of computational thinking were not discussed in the workshop that should be included in subsequent discussions?
— How and to what extent, if any, is the ability to program an essential aspect of computational thinking? What should be the definition of "programming" in this context?

Answers to these questions would provide some structure to computational thinking as a systematized mode of thought. In a 2007 article,[1] Thomas Cortina of Carnegie Mellon University suggests that David Harel's *Algorithmics: The Spirit of Computing*[2] is a good point of departure for developing a coherent structure for how different elements of computational thinking relate to one another.

5.2 HOW CAN A COMPUTATIONAL THINKER BE RECOGNIZED?

Workshop participants grappled with the question of how to determine an individual's competence with computational thinking. Some workshop participants asked how one would determine that a student has mastered basic elements of computational thinking, just as one might master basic reading, writing, or arithmetic skills. Others asked how one might certify teachers as having both competence in computational thinking and the ability to teach computational thinking. In Ursula Wolz's words, "What does it mean to create teachers who have that kind of

---

[1] Thomas Cortina, 2007, "An Introduction to Computer Science for Non-majors Using Principles of Computation," Technical Symposium on Computer Science Education, Proceedings of the 38th SIGCSE Technical Symposium on Computer Science Education, Covington, Kentucky. ACM Special Interest Group on Computer Science Education, March 7-10, 2007, pp. 218-222.

[2] David Harel, 1987, *Algorithmics: The Spirit of Computing*, 1st ed. Reading, Mass.: Addison-Wesley.

literacy, both to read the languages and so that they can think about it and express it to their students, and also so that they become facile writers? . . . to make sure that what we are doing is teaching them how to read and write, not how to do phonics."

Several workshop participants noted the importance of context in computational thinking, expressing the view that just as learning arithmetic goes beyond more than knowing the algorithms of addition and multiplication to being able to apply these algorithms in real-world situations, being a competent computational thinker must include the ability to apply computational thinking to actual problems. That is, even if it is feasible to articulate clearly the content of computational thinking, such content becomes meaningful only in some specific context. One must use computational thinking in a context and must understand the nature of the context to apply computational thinking skills effectively.

The question of generalizability is also important. Experts in one field are not necessarily successful in exploring other fields. Experts may be more facile at learning in related domains than students who are not yet expert in any particular domain, but a lack of understanding of the related domain will limit the success even of experts. So, arguably, another part of computational thinking is the ability to apply its content to multiple domains and to recognize the connections between those applications.

Along these lines, Richard Lipton expressed this sentiment as follows: "The greatest challenge to a computational thinker, to any thinker, is stating the problem in a way that will allow a solution." What are you really trying to accomplish? The ability to recognize when "the same question is being asked" or "the same problem presented" can facilitate use of computational thinking in new disciplines.

5.3 WHAT IS THE CONNECTION BETWEEN TECHNOLOGY AND COMPUTATIONAL THINKING?

Workshop participants were divided on the centrality of technology to computational thinking. Some expressed the view that at its core, computational thinking was independent of technology—that being a competent computational thinker did not necessarily imply anything about one's ability to use modern information technology. Some participants argued that computational thinking is an emergent property of technological advance. As technologies develop they enable new forms of computational thinking. Others believed that the connections between information technology and computational thinking were so deep that it effectively makes no sense to regard the two as separate. In this view, the computer—and notions of computer programming—can make the concepts, principles, methods, models, and tools of computational thinking tangible, in much the same spirit that LOGO was first inspired.

5.4 WHAT IS THE BEST PEDAGOGY FOR PROMOTING COMPUTATIONAL THINKING?

A great deal of education research in recent years suggests (1) that students can learn thinking strategies such as computational thinking as they study a discipline, (2) that teachers and curricula can model these strategies for students, and (3) that appropriate guidance can enable students to learn to use these strategies independently. In many cases, a key element of "appropriate guidance" consists of the capabilities afforded by a suitable computational environment and toolkits, such as programming languages for computing and modeling languages for noncomputing domains that are particularly helpful in promoting computational thinking.

Recent exploratory research on technology-enhanced learning suggests that computers can facilitate this process by guiding students as they explore complex problems, use scientific visualization, and collaborate with peers.[3] Such learning environments may also increase the effectiveness of teachers by synthesizing results from embedded assessments, allowing teachers to monitor progress in real time, and by handling routine tasks.

Exploring these questions will be a major focus of the committee's second workshop.

---

[3] See, for example, Uri Wilensky and Kenneth Reisman, 2006, "Thinking Like a Wolf, a Sheep, or a Firefly: Learning Biology Through Constructing and Testing Computational Theories—an Embodied Modeling Approach," *Cognition and Instruction* 24(2):171-209; Uri Wilensky and Mitchel Resnick, 1999, "Thinking in Levels: A Dynamic Systems Approach to Making Sense of the World," *Journal of Science Education and Technology* 8(1):3-19; Uri Wilensky, 2001, "Modeling Nature's Emergent Patterns with NetLogo," *Proceedings of the Eurologo 2001 Conference*, Linz, Austria; J.L. Kolodner et al., 2003, "Problem-Based Learning Meets Case-Based Reasoning in the Middle-School Science Classroom: Putting Learning by Design into Practice," *Journal of the Learning Sciences* 12(4):495-548; S. Puntambekar and J.L. Kolodner, 2005, "Toward Implementing Distributed Scaffolding: Helping Students Learn Science by Design," *Journal of Research in Science Teaching* 42(2):185-217; Y. Kali and M.C. Linn, 2009, "Designing Effective Visualizations for Elementary School Science," *Elementary School Journal* 109(5):181-198; M.C. Linn, H.S. Lee, R. Tinker, F. Husic, and J.L. Chiu, 2006, "Teaching and Assessing Knowledge Integration in Science," *Science* 313:1049-1050; Y.B. Kafai, 2006, "Playing and Making Games for Learning: Instructionist and Constructionist Perspectives for Game Studies," *Games and Culture* 1(1):36-40; and Y.B. Kafai and C.C. Ching, 2001, "Affordances of Collaborative Software Design Planning for Elementary Students' Science Talk," *Journal of the Learning Sciences* 10(3):323-363. The papers listed in this footnote represent a small fraction of the research performed on technology-enhanced learning in the last decade—what is common to the papers above is that because their authors included, to a considerable extent, members of the NRC committee for the workshop reported in this volume, they were more familiar to the committee.

5.5 WHAT IS THE PROPER INSTITUTIONAL ROLE OF THE COMPUTER SCIENCE COMMUNITY WITH RESPECT TO COMPUTATIONAL THINKING?

Although there is obviously a close (though not fully understood) cognitive and intellectual connection between computational thinking and computer science as a subject of study, the role of computer science as a discipline and as a community of individuals who call themselves computer scientists in defining and structuring the content of computational thinking is much less clear.

For example, Robert Constable noted that today, university-level discussions regarding computational thinking education (or, more precisely, computing) are usually set forward by a department of X that believes in the value of computing as a tool for effective study of X—and thus focus on computational thinking in the context of X. But these efforts rarely focus on the abstractions and concepts that computer scientists believe cut across specific disciplinary applications of computational thinking.

Constable further pointed out that even in colleges of computing and information, the discussion of computational thinking does not always reach out to the entire university. This disconnect occurs despite the attempts of some of these colleges to "teach every undergraduate" about computing and digital information by way of general education requirements.

Given this disconnect, he argued, it is thus not surprising that the development of K-12 computational thinking education has a certain inchoate quality—if the leading schools of computing and departments of computer science don't know how to talk about computational thinking, how can others define the content of "computational thinking for everyone"?

A second issue relates to disciplinary "ownership" of computational thinking. Because computational thinking is a critical skill in many disciplines, there are already a few stakes in the ground from a range of disciplines, such as biology, statistics, and physics. This fact led several workshop participants to note the importance of refraining from turf wars over which disciplines own what with respect to computational thinking.

They felt that there were a number of areas of overlap and that this was a positive sign. These speakers were reassured by the overlap, believing that it might be a strength that everyone wants to claim computational thinking for their own field.

Another set of workshop participants noted concern that a lack of disciplinary ownership could make it difficult to build support and a community sense of responsibility for the education of the next generation. They were concerned that other disciplines claiming ownership of key components of computational thinking can slow its development as a scientific paradigm in and of itself.

Some argued that computational thinking can help advance a number of disciplines and encourage innovation. The inverse situation—lack of deep computational understanding and lack of technical communication skills—might even give rise to the stifling of innovation. This is a key concern according to columnist Adam C. Engst. In the article entitled "Have We Entered a Post-Literate Technological Age?" he states, "My more serious concern with our society's odd fluency with a technology that we cannot easily communicate about is that it might slowly stifle innovation."[4] As an example, he notes that a person who is able to fluidly navigate an application does not necessarily understand anything about what is going on underneath the hood.

Others argued that computational thinking is inherently multidisciplinary. To engage in computational thinking, one must reason about something. By claiming that computational thinking can benefit all disciplines, one endorses the idea that computational thinking will evolve as it is used in varied disciplines. In addition, the disciplines using computational thinking will develop in novel directions as a result of using computational thinking.

---

[4] Adam C. Engst, 2009, "Have We Entered a Post-Literate Technological Age?" August 18, TidBITS.com. Available at http://db.tidbits.com/article/10493.

6

Next Steps

Discussions held at the February 2009 workshop did not reveal general agreement among workshop participants about the precise content of computational thinking, let alone its structure. Nevertheless, the lack of explicit disagreement about its elements could be taken as reflecting a shared intuition among workshop participants that computational thinking, as a mode of thought, has its own distinctive character.

Building on this shared intuition, it is fair to say that most workshop participants agreed that more deliberation is necessary to achieve greater clarity about what is encompassed under the rubric of computational thinking and how these elements are structured relative to each other. Toward this end, workshop participants thought that the second workshop would have value. Scheduled to occur in early 2010 and devoted to exploring pedagogy and how best to expose students to the ideas of computational thinking, the deliberations of this follow-on workshop will be valuable in shedding additional light on the content and structure of computational thinking for three reasons.

First, the diversity of views on the nature of computational thinking allows a great deal for exploration and innovation within the boundaries of a shared intuition, even if that intuition was not made precise in the first workshop.

Second, when designing courses, educators often reveal their beliefs about what is central to the subjects in question. Thus, a consideration of provocative and innovative examples of courses and curricular material related to computational thinking is likely to provide valuable further insights into individual perspectives on that topic.

Last, and as noted at the end of Section 4.1.1, the technological substrate has proliferated by orders of magnitude since the late 1960s. Young people today—the targets of K-12 education—are correspondingly far more familiar with various manifestations of information technology and thus also more familiar with different contexts in which computational thinking can be relevant. It is hoped that the pedagogical focus of the second workshop will shed additional light on some of these different contexts.

For these reasons, the committee looks forward to the second workshop with anticipation.

Appendixes

A

Workshop Agenda

FEBRUARY 19, 2009

8:30-8:45 AM **Welcome and Housekeeping**
Marcia Linn, University of California, Berkeley, Committee Chair

8:45-10:30 AM **Panel 1—The Scope and Nature of Computational Thinking**

- How is computational thinking different from mathematical thinking?
- How is it different from quantitative reasoning?
- How is it different from scientific thinking?
- How is it different from fluency with information technology?

Presenters:
Jeannette Wing, National Science Foundation
Wm. Wulf, University of Virginia
Gerald Sussman, Massachusetts Institute of Technology
Peter Lee, Carnegie Mellon University

Committee respondent: *Larry Snyder*

10:30-12:15 PM **Panel 2—Computational Thinking Everywhere (Part I)**

- What kinds of problems require computational thinking? What are some examples?
- How, if at all, does computational thinking vary by discipline? What would be the nature of computational thinking for physicists, biologists, engineers, lawyers, physicians, historians, sociologists, teachers, accountants, homemakers, bus drivers, and so on?
- What are the exposures and experiences needed to develop the level of computational thinking needed in various disciplines?
- What are contemporary issues facing the nation that would benefit from greater development of computational thinking?
- What is the value of computational thinking for nonscientists?
- How, if at all, would widespread facility with computational thinking enhance the productivity of U.S. workers?
- How do we best illustrate the power of computational thinking?

Presenters:
Kevin Ashley, University of Pittsburgh
Chris Hoffmann, Purdue University
Alan Kay, Viewpoints Research Institute, Inc.
Richard Lipton, Georgia Tech
Robert Sproull, Sun Microsystems, Inc.

Committee respondent: *M. Brian Blake*

12:15-1:15 PM **Working Lunch—Other Related Ongoing Efforts**

Andrew Bernat: CRA Education Committee
Peter Denning: Great Principles of Computing (via videoconference)

APPENDIX A

1:15-3:00 PM	**Panel 3—Computational Thinking Everywhere (Part II)**

Presenters:

> Andrew McGettrick, University of Strathclyde (invited)
> Edward Fox, Virginia Tech
> Ian Foster, Argonne National Laboratory/University of Chicago (via conference call)
> Paulo Blikstein, Northwestern University
> Eric Roberts, Stanford University

Committee respondent: *Robert Constable*

3:00-3:10 PM	**Break**
3:10-4:40 PM	**Panel 4—Technology and Computational Thinking (Show and Tell)**

- What affordances are provided by new technologies for computational thinking?
- What is the role of information technology in imparting computational thinking skills?
- What parts of computational thinking can be taught without the use of computers? Without the skills of computer programming?

Participants:
> Mitchel Resnick, Massachusetts Institute of Technology
> Ken Kahn, Oxford University
> David Moursund, University of Oregon

Committee respondent: *Janet Kolodner*

4:40-4:45 PM	**Break**
4:45-5:15 PM	**Other Related Ongoing Efforts** *Tim Bell, New Zealand Computer Science Unplugged (via videoconference)*
5:15-5:30 PM	**Wrap-up**
5:30	**Adjourn Day-One Public Sessions**

5:30-6:15 PM   **Reception**

6:15-8:15 PM   **Working Dinner in Small Groups**

- Homework assignment—What is the core of computational thinking? What are the fundamental principles of computational thinking? What concepts are derivative from the fundamentals?
- Are there multiple decompositions of computational thinking into fundamental and derivative parts? What are some examples?
- How, if at all, can computational thinking be decomposed into an intellectual hierarchy?

FEBRUARY 20, 2009

8:30-8:35 AM   **Welcome and Housekeeping**
Marcia Linn, University of Berkeley, Committee Chair

8:35-10:00 AM   **Panel 5—Report-back on homework assignments:**

Committee respondent: *Alfred Aho*

10:00-10:15 AM   **Break**

10:15-11:45 AM   **Panel 6—Bridging into Education**

- Are the fundamental principles of computational thinking the easiest to grasp? If so, why? If not, why not?
- Are the fundamental principles the logical starting point for the teaching of computational thinking? If so, why? If not, why not?

Participants:
Dor Abrahamson,University of California, Berkeley
Owen Astrachan, Duke University
Lenore Blum, Carnegie Mellon University
Andy diSessa, University of California, Berkeley

Committee respondent: *Uri Wilensky*

11:45-12:45 PM	**Working Lunch—Computer Science Advanced Placement Efforts** *Jan Cuny, National Science Foundation*
12:45-2:15 PM	**Panel 7—Related Best Practices in Teaching/Pedagogy**

- How do we engage all learners in computational thinking?
- What are the exposures and experiences needed to develop computational thinking?
- What is the role of the computer in instruction? Where does programming fit into computational thinking?

Presenters:
Roy Pea, Stanford University
Allan Collins, Northwestern University
Ursula Wolz, The College of New Jersey
Joshua Danish, Indiana University

Committee respondent: *Yasmin Kafai*

2:15-2:30 PM	**Break**
2:30-4:30 PM	**Discussion and Wrap-up**

- Committee members summarize their individual reactions
- Floor opened to other workshop participants

4:30 PM	**Adjourn**

B

Short Biographies of Committee Members, Workshop Participants, and Staff

B.1 COMMITTEE

Marcia C. Linn (*Chair*) is a professor specializing in education in mathematics, science, and technology in the Graduate School of Education at the University of California, Berkeley. She directs the NSF-funded Technology-Enhanced Learning in Science (TELS) center. She is a member of the National Academy of Education and a fellow of the American Association for the Advancement of Science, the American Psychological Association, and the Center for Advanced Study in Behavioral Sciences. Board service includes the American Association for the Advancement of Science board, the Graduate Record Examination Board of the Educational Testing Service, the McDonnell Foundation Cognitive Studies in Education Practice board, and the Education and Human Resources Directorate at the National Science Foundation. Linn earned a Ph.D. in educational psychology from Stanford University.

Alfred V. Aho (NAE) is the Lawrence Gussman Professor of Computer Science and vice chair of undergraduate education for the Computer Science Department at Columbia University. Previously, he conducted research at Bell Laboratories from 1963 to 1991, and again from 1997 to 2002 as vice president of the Computing Sciences Research Center. Aho's current research interests include quantum computing, programming languages, compilers, and algorithms. He is part of the Language and Compilers research group at Columbia. He is widely known for his development of the AWK programming language with Peter J. Weinberger and Brian

Kernighan (the "A" stands for "Aho"), and for his co-authorship of *Compilers: Principles, Techniques, and Tools* (the "Dragon book") with Ravi Sethi and Jeffrey Ullman. He wrote the initial versions of the Unix tools egrep and fgrep. He is also a co-author (along with Jeffrey Ullman and John Hopcroft) of a number of widely used textbooks on several areas of computer science, including algorithms and data structures, and the foundations of computer science. He is a past president of ACM's Special Interest Group on Algorithms and Computability Theory. Aho has chaired the Advisory Committee for the Computer and Information Sciences Directorate of the National Science Foundation. He has received many prestigious honors, including the IEEE's John von Neumann Medal and membership in the American Academy of Arts and Sciences. Aho was elected to the National Academy of Engineering in 1999 for contributions to the fields of algorithms and programming tools. Aho earned his Ph.D. in electrical engineering and computer science from Princeton University.

M. Brian Blake is a professor of computer science and associate dean of engineering at the University of Notre Dame. His research interests include the investigation of automated approaches to sharing information and software capabilities across organization boundaries, sometimes referred to as enterprise integration. His investigations cover the spectrum of software engineering: design, specification, proof of correctness, implementation/experimentation, performance evaluation, and application. Blake's long-term vision is the creation of adaptable software entities or software agents that can be deployed on the Internet and, using existing resources, can manage the creation of new processes, sometimes referred to as interorganizational workflow. He has several ongoing projects that make incremental progress toward this long-term vision. In addition, he conducts experimentation in the areas of software engineering education and software process and improvement to determine the most effective methods for training students and professionals to develop module systems that by nature are distributed. Blake has consulted for such companies as General Electric, Lockheed Martin, General Dynamics, and the MITRE Corporation. He has published more than 95 refereed journal papers and conference proceedings in the areas of service-oriented computing, agents and workflow, enterprise integration, component-based software engineering, distributed data management, and software engineering education. Blake's work has been funded by the Federal Aviation Administration, the MITRE Corporation, the National Science Foundation, DARPA, the Air Force Research Laboratory, SAIC, and the National Institutes of Health. He earned his doctorate in information technology and computer science from George Mason University.

Robert Constable is the dean of the Faculty of Computing and Information Science at Cornell University. Formerly he was the chair of the Computer Science Department for 6 years. He also heads a research group in automated reasoning and formal methods in the Computer Science Department, where he is a professor. Constable is a graduate of Princeton University, where he worked with Alonzo Church, one of the pioneers of computer science. He did his Ph.D. work at the University of Wisconsin with Stephen Cole Kleene, a Ph.D. student of Church and another pioneer of computer science. Church traces his mathematical lineage back to Gottfried Wilhelm Leibniz, one of the first logicians interested in mechanical computation and the digitization of human knowledge. Constable joined the Cornell University faculty in 1968. He has supervised more than 43 Ph.D. students in computer science. He is known for work in connecting programs and mathematical proofs that has led to new ways of automating the production of reliable software. This work is known by the slogan "proofs as programs," and it is embodied in the Nuprl ("new pearl") theorem prover. He has written three books on this topic as well as numerous research articles. Since 1980 he has headed a project that uses Nuprl to design and verify software systems, instances of which are still operational in industry and science. Currently he is working on extending this programming method to concurrent processes, realizing the notion of "proofs as processes." In 1999 he became the first dean of the Faculty of Computing and Information Science, a unit that includes the Computer Science Department, the Department of Statistical Science, the Information Science Program, and the Program in Computer Graphics. It also sponsors the undergraduate major and graduate field in computational biology.

Yasmin B. Kafai is a professor at the Graduate School of Education, University of Pennsylvania. In addition, she spent more than a decade on the faculty at the UCLA Graduate School of Education and Information Studies. As a learning scientist, she has researched and developed media-rich software tools and environments—most recently Scratch, together with researchers at the MIT Media Lab—that support youth in schools and community centers in becoming designers of games, simulations, and virtual worlds. As part of her policy initiatives, she wrote *Under the Microscope: A Decade of Gender Equity Interventions in the Sciences* (2004) and participated in the national commission that produced the report *Tech-Savvy Girls: Educating Girls in the Computer Age* (2000) for the American Association of University Women. She also briefed the Computer Science and Telecommunications National Research Council report *Being Fluent with Information Technology* (National Academy Press, Washington, D.C., 1999). While conducting research at the Massachusetts Institute of Technology Media Laboratory, she received her Ed.D. in human development and psychology from Harvard University.

Janet L. Kolodner is a Regents' Professor in the School of Interactive Computing at Georgia Institute of Technology. Her research over the past 30 years has addressed a wide variety of issues in learning, memory, and problem solving, both in computers and in people. During the 1980s, she pioneered the computer method called case-based reasoning, which allows a computer to reason and learn from its experiences. The first case-based design aids (CBDAs) came from her lab. Archie-2, for example, helped architecture students with conceptual design. During the early 1990s, she used the cognitive model implied by case-based reasoning to address issues in creative design. JULIA planned meals, Creative JULIA figured out what to do with leftover rice, IMPROVISOR did simple mechanical design, and ALEC simulated Alexander Graham Bell in his invention of the telephone. Later in the 1990s, she used the cognitive model in case-based reasoning to guide the design of a science curriculum for middle school. Learning by Design™ is a design-based learning approach and an inquiry-oriented project-based approach to science learning that has children learn science from their design experiences. The sequencing of activities in the classroom encourages students to reflect on their design and science experiences in ways that case-based reasoning says are appropriate for integrating them well into memory. Learning by Design curriculum units and the sequencing structures in Learning by Design are being integrated into a full 3-year middle-school science curriculum called Project-Based Inquiry Science (PBIS). Most recently, Kolodner's research uses what she learned in designing Learning by Design to create informal learning environments to help middle schoolers come to think of themselves as competent scientific reasoners. In Kitchen Science Investigators, fifth and sixth graders learn science in the context of cooking. In Hovering Around, they learn about motion and forces, about airflow, and about how to explain in the context of designing hovercraft. Kolodner is founding editor in chief of the *Journal of the Learning Sciences* and is a founder and first executive officer of the International Society for the Learning Sciences. She has headed up the Cognitive Science Program at Georgia Tech and headed an organization called EduTech in the mid-1990s whose mission was to use what is known about cognition to design educational software and integrate it appropriately into educational environments. She has a B.S. from Brandeis University in math and computer science and an M.S. and a Ph.D. in computer science from Yale University.

Lawrence Snyder is a professor of computer science and engineering at the University of Washington in Seattle. Snyder's research has focused on parallel computation, including architecture, algorithms, and languages. He has served on the faculties of Yale and Purdue universities and has had visiting appointments at UW, Harvard, MIT, Sydney University, the Swiss Technological University, the University of Auckland, and Kyoto University. In 1980 he invented programmable interconnect, a method to dynamically configure on-chip components, and a technology used today for FPGAs. In 1990 he was co-designer of Chaos Router, a randomizing adaptive packet router. He was the principal investigator of the ZPL language design project, the first high-level parallel language to achieve "performance portability" across all parallel computer platforms. Snyder is the author of *Fluency with Information Technology: Skills, Concepts and Capabilities*, a textbook for non-techie college freshmen that teaches fundamental computing concepts; the book is in its third edition. With former Ph.D. student Calvin Lin (University of Texas, Austin), he has written *Principles of Parallel Programming*, published in 2008. Snyder was a three-term member of the Computer Research Association Board of Directors, developing a series of best-practices white papers. He chaired the NSF CISE Advisory Board as well as several CISE directorate oversight panels and numerous review panels. The two National Research Council studies that he chaired produced influential reports—*Academic Careers for Experimental Computer Scientists and Engineers* (1994) and *Being Fluent with Information Technology* (1999). He served three terms on the NRC's Army Research Laboratory Technical Advisory Board. He serves on ACM's Education Board, has been general chair or program committee chair of several ACM and IEEE conferences, and is a fellow of both the ACM and the IEEE. He received a B.A. from the University of Iowa in mathematics and economics and his Ph.D. from Carnegie Mellon University as a student of A. Nico Habermann.

Uri Wilensky is a professor of learning sciences and computer science at Northwestern University and holds appointments in the cognitive science program and in complex systems. He is the founder and current director of the Center for Connected Learning and Computer-Based Modeling and also a founder and member of the governing board of the Northwestern Institute on Complex Systems (NICO). His most recent projects focus on developing tools that enable users (both researchers and learners) to simulate, explore, and make sense of complex systems. His NetLogo agent-based modeling software is in widespread use worldwide. Prior to coming to Northwestern, he taught at Tufts University and MIT and was a research scientist at Thinking Machines Corporation. Wilensky is a founder and an executive editor of the *International Journal of Computers for Mathematical Learning*. His research interests include computer-based modeling and agent-based modeling, STEM education, mathematics in the context of computation, and complex systems. He is a recipient of the National Science Foundation's Career Award as well as the Spencer Foundation's Post-Doctoral Award. He has directed numerous NSF research projects focused on developing computer-based modeling tools and studying their use. Among these tools are multi-agent modeling languages such as StarLogoT and NetLogo, model-based curricula such as GasLab, ProbLab, NIELS, and BEAGLE Evolution, and Participatory Simulation Toolkits such as Calc-HubNet and Computer-HubNet. The tools enable learners to explore and create simulations of complex phenomena across many domains of the natural and social sciences and, through creating and exploring such simulations, deepen their understanding of core scientific concepts. Many of these tools are also in use by researchers across a wide variety of domains including the natural sciences, social sciences, business, and medicine. By providing a "low-threshold" language for exploring and constructing models, Wilensky hopes to promote modeling literacy—the sharing and critiquing of models in the scientific community, in education, and in the public at large. Wilensky did his undergraduate and graduate studies in mathematics, philosophy, and computer science at Brandeis and Harvard universities and received his Ph.D. in media arts and sciences from the Massachusetts Institute of Technology.

B.2 WORKSHOP PARTICIPANTS

Dor Abrahamson specializes in the study of mathematical intuition, reasoning, and learning from the synergistic perspectives of cognitive and sociocultural theory. He investigates in particular the roles that mediated, reflexive interaction with a range of technologies plays in students' content-focused and intellectual development, which he views as trajectories from intuition to inscription. A core aspect of Abrahamson's professional practice is the design, production, implementation, and evaluation of innovative mixed-media concept-targeted curricular artifacts aligned with the emerging empiricism of individual cognition in social context. Operating in design-based research methodology, Abrahamson is particularly interested in instances of spontaneous multimodal coordination of distributed epistemic and material resources and in the roles of teachers in facilitating conceptual insight. Abrahamson also explores the impact of complexity studies' perspectives and methodologies on education research and has been arguing for the use of agent-based modeling to advance theories of individual learning in social context. During his tenure as a Spencer Postdoctoral Fellow, Abrahamson developed computer-based modules for learning probability. He has published in the *Handbook of Mathematical Cognition*, *International Journal of Computers for Mathematical Learning* (and is a member of the editorial board), *Educational Studies in Mathematics*,

Cognition & Instruction, For the Learning of Mathematics, Mathematics Teaching in the Middle School, and the *Journal of Statistics Education,* and he contributes regularly to major international conferences. He received his M.A. in cognitive psychology in 2000 from Tel Aviv University, Israel, and a Ph.D. in learning sciences in 2004 from Northwestern University.

Kevin Ashley holds interdisciplinary appointments as a faculty member of the Graduate Program in Intelligent Systems at the University of Pittsburgh, a senior scientist at the Learning Research and Development Center, a professor of law, and an adjunct professor of computer science. His goals are to contribute to artificial intelligence (AI) research on case-based and analogical reasoning, argumentation, and explanation and to develop instructional and information retrieval systems for professionals in case-based domains such as law and ethics. Currently, he and his students are pursuing research projects in automatically indexing legal case texts, engaging law students in online argumentation dialogues, intelligent retrieval of ethics codes and cases, and Web-based tutoring to help students get more from reading ethics cases. For his Ph.D., he developed an AI CBR system, HYPO, which reasons by analogy to past legal cases, makes arguments about legal fact situations, and poses hypothetical cases. MIT Press/Bradford Books published his book, based on his dissertation, entitled *Modeling Legal Argument: Reasoning with Cases and Hypotheticals.* In April 1990, the National Science Foundation selected Professor Ashley as a Presidential Young Investigator, and in 2002 he was selected as a fellow of the American Association of Artificial Intelligence. From June 1988 through July 1989, he was a visiting scientist at the Thomas J. Watson Research Center, Yorktown Heights, New York. For 4 years prior to his computer science graduate work, he was an associate attorney at White & Case, a large Wall Street law firm. While a philosophy major at Princeton, he was a research assistant for Professor Walter Kaufmann. He received a B.A. in philosophy (magna cum laude) from Princeton University in 1973, a J.D. (cum laude) from Harvard Law School in 1976, and a Ph.D. in computer science in 1988 from the University of Massachusetts, where he held an IBM Graduate Research Fellowship.

Owen Astrachan is a professor of the practice of computer science at Duke University and the department's director of undergraduate studies for teaching and learning. He received an NSF CAREER award in 1997 to incorporate design patterns in undergraduate computer science curricula, received an IBM Faculty Award in 2004 to support componentization in both software and curricula, and was one of two inaugural NSF CISE Distinguished Education Fellows in 2007, awarded to revitalize computer science education using case- and problem-based learning. Astrachan's research interests have been built on understanding how best to teach and learn about object-oriented programming, software design, and computer science in general; he is now working on developing a portfolio of substantial, interdisciplinary problems that help explain how computer science is relevant to students in the social and natural sciences. Astrachan received Duke University's 1995 Robert B. Cox Distinguished Teaching in Science Award, an Outstanding Instructor Award while teaching on sabbatical at the University of British Columbia in 1998, and Duke's 2002 Richard K. Lublin Award for "ability to engender genuine intellectual excitement, ability to engender curiosity, knowledge of the field and ability to communicate that knowledge." He earned his A.B. degree with distinction in mathematics from Dartmouth and an MAT (Math), an M.S., and a Ph.D. in computer science from Duke.

Tim Bell is an associate professor in the Department of Computer Science and Software Engineering at the University of Canterbury in Christchurch, New Zealand. His current research interests include computers and music, public understanding of (computer) science, and educational applications of podcasting. He received the Science Communicator Award from the NZ Association of Scientists in 1999, and an inaugural New Zealand Tertiary Teaching Excellence Award in 2002. He has appeared with his "Computer Science Unplugged" show at the Edinburgh International Science Festival, the Dunedin International Science Festival, and the Australian Science Festival. He is also a qualified musician and performs regularly on instruments that have black-and-white keyboards. He is co-author of the books *Text Compression* and *Managing Gigabytes*.

Andrew Bernat was a founding member and chair of the Computer Science Department at the University of Texas at El Paso (spending 20 years there) and a former NSF program director. He is currently the executive director of the Computing Research Association, whose mission is to strengthen research and education in the computing fields, expand opportunities for women and minorities, and improve the public's and policy makers' understanding of the importance of computing and computing research in our society. In recognition of "his success in creating arguably the strongest computer science department at a minority-serving institution," the Computing Research Association honored him with the 1997 A. Nico Habermann Award.

Paulo Blikstein is an assistant professor at Stanford University's School of Education, with a courtesy appointment in the Computer Science Department. His research focuses on computational literacy, low-cost educational technologies for low-income settings, and STEM education. His work cuts across age groups—he has worked extensively with inner-city students in developing countries, such as Brazil, Mexico, Senegal, and Costa Rica, but also with undergraduates in elite U.S. institutions. His research tries to bring the most cutting-edge computational tools to the classroom, creating environments for students to authentically engage in advanced, deep scientific inquiry.

Lenore Blum is Distinguished Career Professor of Computer Science at Carnegie Mellon University, where she co-directs the ALADDIN Center for Algorithm Adaptation, Dissemination and Integration, is a faculty advisor to the student organization Women@SCS, and is the principal investigator for the Google-funded CS4HS program for high school teachers. Her most recent creation and passion is Project Olympus, a high-tech innovation center that she directs at Carnegie Mellon. In 2009, the impact of this work was acknowledged by the Carnegie Science "Catalyst" award. Blum's research, from her early work in model theory and differential fields (logic and algebra) to her more recent work in developing a theory of computation and complexity over the real numbers (mathematics and computer science), has focused on merging seemingly unrelated areas. She received her doctorate in mathematics from MIT the same year that Princeton University first allowed women to enter its graduate program. She then taught at the University of California, Berkeley, and at Mills College, where she founded the Department of Mathematics and Computer Science (the first computer science department at a women's college), served as its head or co-head for 13 years, and became the first holder of the Letts-Villard Chair. In 1988 she joined the Theory Group of the newly formed International Computer Science Institute in Berkeley and from 1992 to 1996 also served as deputy director of the Mathematical Sciences Research Institute. Blum spent 2 years, 1996-1998, spanning the historic handover of Hong Kong from Britain to China, at CityU of Hong Kong as a visiting professor of mathematics and computer science, and she completed her book, *Complexity and Real Computation*, there with her colleagues. She has served the professional community in numerous capacities, including as president of the Association for Women in Mathematics, as vice president of the American Mathematical Society, and as a member of numerous committees, including the MIT Visiting Committee for Mathematics and the ACM SIGACT Committee for the Advancement of Theoretical Computer Science. She is a fellow of the American Association for the Advancement of Science. She received her Ph.D. in mathematics from MIT in 1968.

Allan Collins is a professor emeritus of education and social policy at Northwestern University. He is a member of the National Academy of Education and a fellow of the American Association for Artificial Intelligence, the Cognitive Science Society, the American Educational Research Association, and the American Association for the Advancement of Science. He served as a founding editor of the journal *Cognitive Science* and as first chair of the Cognitive Science Society. He has studied teaching and learning for more than 30 years and has written extensively on related topics. He is best known in psychology for his work on how people answer questions, in artificial intelligence for his work on reasoning and intelligent tutoring systems, and in education for his work on situated learning, inquiry teaching, design research, and cognitive apprenticeship. From 1991 to 1994 he was co-director of the U.S. Department of Education's Center for Technology in Education.

Jan Cuny is a program officer at the National Science Foundation, heading the Broadening Participation in Computing program. Before coming to NSF in 2004, she was a faculty member in computer science at Purdue University, the University of Massachusetts, and the University of Oregon. Cuny has been involved for many years in efforts to increase the participation of women in computing research. She was a longtime member of the Computing Research Association's Committee on the Status of Women (CRA-W), serving, among other activities, as a CRA-W co-chair, a mentor in its Distributed Mentoring program, and a lead on its Academic Career Mentoring Workshop, Grad Cohort, and Cohort for Associated Professors projects. She was also a member of the Advisory Board for the Anita Borg Institute for Women and Technology, the leadership team of the National Center for Women in Technology, the executive committee of the Coalition to Diversify Computing, and the ACM Education Council. She was program chair of the 2004 Grace Hopper Conference and the general chair of the 2006 conference. For her efforts with underserved populations, Cuny was a recipient of one of the 2006 ACM President's Awards and the CRA's 2007 A. Nico Habermann Award.

Joshua Danish's research examines the role of external representations, such as drawings, maps, and computer simulations, in supporting cognition and learning. To study learning and development in classroom contexts, he employs cultural historical activity theory to articulate the influence of various mediators—the physical tools, rules, division of labor, and local community—on students' activities as they learn and develop. Recent research has included the development and study of BeeSign, a computer simulation and accompanying curriculum that engages kindergarten and first-grade students in learning about the nectar-gathering behavior of honeybee hives; the Community Mapping Project, in which seventh-grade students learned basic statistics concepts using the MyWorld Geographical Information Systems mapping software to study local community issues; and the Semiotic Pivots and Activity Spaces for Elementary Science project, which takes advantage of sensing technologies and augmented reality tools to support first- and second-grade students in learning about physical science concepts.

Peter J. Denning is a Distinguished Professor at the Naval Postgraduate School in Monterey, California. He chairs the Computer Science Department and directs the Cebrowski Institute, an interdisciplinary research center for innovation and information superiority. In the 1990s he was at George Mason University, where he was vice provost, associate dean, Computer Science Department chair, and founder of the Center for the New Engineer. In the 1980s, he was the founding director of the Research Institute for Advanced Computer Science at NASA-Ames and was co-founder of CSNET. He received a Ph.D. from MIT and a B.E.E. from Manhattan College. He was president of the Association for Computing Machinery (ACM) in 1980-1982. As chair of the ACM publications board in 1992-1998, he was project leader for the ACM digital library, now the ACM's crown jewel. In 1967 he discovered the locality principle for referencing storage objects and used it to invent the influential working set model for program behavior; his original paper was named to the ACM SIGOPS Hall of Fame in 2005. He helped establish virtual memory as a permanent part of operating systems. He contributed important extensions to operational analysis, an approach to computer system performance prediction. He leads the Great Principles of Computing project, which is identifying the scientific theories of computing and applying them to curriculum innovation. He also co-leads an Innovation project that has identified and teaches the seven foundational practices of innovation. He has published seven books and 315 articles on computers, networks, and their operating systems. He is working on two more books, one on the foundational practices of innovation and the other on the great principles of computing. In 2002, he was named one of the top five best teachers at George Mason University and the best teacher in the School of Information Technology and Engineering. In 2003, he received one of Virginia's 10 outstanding faculty awards. He holds three honorary degrees, three professional society fellowships, two best-paper awards, three distinguished service awards, the ACM Outstanding Contribution Award, the ACM SIGCSE Outstanding CS Educator Award, and the prestigious ACM Karl Karlstrom Outstanding Educator Award. In 2007 ACM gave him a special award for 40 years of continuous volunteer service, and the NSF gave him one of two Distinguished Education Fellow awards.

Andrea diSessa is the Corey Professor of Education and a member of the National Academy of Education. His research centers on conceptual and experiential knowledge in physics, and large-scale and deep implications of the use of computers in education ("new literacies"). His current work focuses on student ideas concerning patterns of behavior and control—aka dynamical systems theory. He was a fellow at the Center for Advanced Study in the Behavioral Sciences in 1997-1998 and 2007-2008. He wrote the books *Changing Minds: Computers, Learning and Literacy* (2000) and *Turtle Geometry: The Computer as a Medium for Exploring Mathematics* (with H. Abelson, 1981), and he edited the volume *Computers and Exploratory Learning* (with C. Hoyles, R. Noss, and L. Edwards, 1995). He received his Ph.D. in physics from MIT, and an A.B., also in physics, from Princeton University.

Ian Foster has been appointed director of the Computation Institute. The Computation Institute was created by the University of Chicago and Argonne National Laboratory in 1999 in recognition of the increasingly central role that computation plays in many disciplines of the sciences, medicine, and the humanities. Foster joined Argonne's Mathematics and Computer Science Division in 1989 and has most recently served as associate division director and senior scientist. He is also the Arthur Holly Compton Distinguished Service Professor of Computer Science at the University of Chicago. His research interests are in distributed and parallel computing, and computational science. He has published six books and more than 300 articles and technical reports in these areas. The Distributed Systems Laboratory that he heads at Argonne and Chicago pursues research in these areas and also development of the Globus toolkit, open-source Grid software used widely in business and science.

Edward Fox, after almost a year devoted to running the computer operations at the International Institute for Tropical Agriculture, Ibadan, Nigeria, started teaching at Virginia Tech in 1983. Since 1987 he has worked on electronic theses and dissertations; he is executive director of the Networked Digital Library of Theses and Dissertations. His research, teaching, and service have focused on information, including searching, multimedia/hypertext, and digital libraries. Fox is starting his 103rd funded research grant; these have included working with many disciplines, including animal care, archeology, auto parts, chemistry, electronic publishing, fisheries, geography, gerontology, health, library and information science, physics, and sociology. Two current NSF grants supporting education include (1) "Living in the Knowledge Society (LIKES)," which promotes connecting computing with all other disciplines to ensure better preparation of college students, and (2) "Ensemble," an NSDL pathways project that aims to help "K-gray" learning related to computing. Fox completed his B.S. in electrical engineering and computer science in 1972 at MIT. He also pursued graduate degrees in information retrieval at Cornell University from 1978 to 1982.

Christopher Hoffmann is well known for his work in geometric computing and geometric constraint solving. The simulations of the 9/11 attacks on the Pentagon and on the WTC-1 building generated worldwide media attention. His current projects include shape modeling for traumatic brain injury simulations, and the NSF-supported SECANT project teaching computational thinking to science majors.

Ken Kahn is a senior researcher at Oxford University and the London Knowledge Laboratory. His interest in programming languages for children was sparked while he was a Ph.D. student at the MIT AI Laboratory in the 1970s. While at the MIT AI Lab, he worked with Seymour Papert and others in the Logo Group. After 15 years as a researcher in programming languages and AI, he returned to children's programming languages when he founded Animated Programs to develop ToonTalk. ToonTalk is an advanced programming language that looks like a video game. Children as young as 3 have successfully used it to create programs by training virtual robots to do actions such as giving birds messages to deliver, loading up trucks, and putting things in boxes. Kahn participated in two large-scale European projects in which children built computer games using ToonTalk. More recently he has been designing and building construction kits that enable students to build computer simulations by composing transparent modules.

Alan Kay, president of Viewpoints Research Institute, Inc., is one of the earliest pioneers of object-oriented programming, personal computing, and graphical user interfaces. His contributions have been recognized with the Charles Stark Draper Prize of the National Academy of Engineering "for the vision, conception, and development of the first practical networked personal computers"; the Alan. M. Turing Award from the Association for Computing Machinery "for pioneering many of the ideas at the root of contemporary object-oriented programming languages, leading the team that developed Smalltalk, and for fundamental contributions to personal computing"; and the Kyoto Prize from the Inamori Foundation "for creation of the concept of modern personal computing and contribution to its realization." This work was done in the rich context of the Advanced Research Projects Agency (ARPA) and the Xerox Palo Alto Research Center (PARC) with many talented colleagues. He is an elected fellow of NAE and AAAS, as well as a member of RSA, ACM, and CHM. At Viewpoints Research Institute he and his colleagues continue to explore advanced systems and programming design by aiming for a "Moore's law" advance in software creation of several orders of magnitude. Kay and Viewpoints are also deeply involved in the One Laptop Per Child initiative that seeks to create a Dynabook-like "$100 laptop" for every child in the world (especially in the third world). Kay has a B.A. in mathematics and biology, with minor concentrations in English and anthropology, from the University of Colorado, 1966. He also holds an M.S. and a Ph.D. in computer science (1968 and 1969, both with distinction) from the University of Utah.

Peter Lee is the head of the Computer Science Department at Carnegie Mellon University. In this capacity, he oversees a computing organization whose research and education programs are consistently ranked among the top four in the nation. Prior to assuming his current position, Lee was the vice provost for research, providing administrative oversight and strategic guidance for Carnegie Mellon's research activities, an enterprise that exceeds $400 million annually in sponsored research. Lee is an active researcher, educator, administrator, and servant to the academic community. For his research, he has received several awards, including the ACM SIGOPS Hall of Fame Award, and election as an ACM Fellow. He is a member of the board of directors of the Computing Research Association (where he chairs the Government Affairs Committee), the Computing Community Consortium Council, the Computer Science and Telecommunications Board of the National Research Council, and the DARPA Information Science and Technology Board (of which he is the vice chair).

Richard Lipton is a member of the National Academy of Engineering. His professional career has been primarily in academia. He held faculty appointments at Yale University, the University of California, Berkeley, and Princeton University before joining the faculty in the college of Computing at Georgia Tech. In addition to his computer science academic appointments, Lipton was the founding director of a computer science research laboratory for the Panasonic Corporation and is currently a chief consulting scientist at Telcordia (formerly known as Bellcore). Lipton's research is focused primarily, but not exclusively, on theory. In a recent paper on the power of automata-based proof systems, he explored one way to address the NP = co-NP questions that considered the length of proofs of tautologies in various proof systems. In this joint work with A. Viglas he considered proof systems defined by appropriate classes of automata. Lipton found that in general, starting from a given class of automata, it was possible to define a corresponding proof system in a natural way. One new and more powerful proof system was based on the class of push-down automata. In this work, Lipton presented an exponential lower bound for oblivious read-once branching programs that resulted in a proof system more powerful than oblivious regular resolution. He has also made important contributions in the areas of program testing, software engineering, and, most recently, DNA computing, combining molecular biology and computer science. It is generally acknowledged that Richard Lipton was one of the original pioneers in the field of DNA computing, along with Len Adleman.

Andrew McGettrick studied pure mathematics at the University of Glasgow. He was awarded a scholarship to Peterhouse, Cambridge, obtaining his Ph.D. in pure mathematics and, later, Diploma in computer science. Throughout his career he has been at the University of Strathclyde; he was promoted to professor in 1984 and served for many years as the head of the Department of Computer and Information Sciences. He is a fellow of the Royal Society of Edinburgh, of the Institution of Engineering and Technology, and of the British Computer Society, where he is also vice president, Qualifications and Standards. McGettrick is the chair of the ACM Education Board and Education Council, which provides curriculum guidelines for the key subdisciplines of computing. He also chairs the IET/BCS Competency Liaison Group. McGettrick holds the ACM SIGCSE Award for Lifetime Service.

David Moursund is professor emeritus at the University of Oregon. He founded the International Society for Technology in Education and served as its executive officer for 19 years. He served 6 years as the first head of the Computer Science Department at the University of Oregon. He is the major or co-major professor of six Ph.D. students in mathematics and 70 in the College of Education. He is the author or co-author of more than 50 books and more than 200 articles. Currently, Moursund runs a nonprofit organization named Information Age Education. Its activities include a Wiki, a website, and a free twice-a-month newsletter. He received his doctorate in mathematics from the University of Wisconsin-Madison.

Roy Pea is Stanford University Professor of the Learning Sciences and director of the Stanford Center for Innovations in Learning. He has published widely on such topics as distributed cognition, learning, and education fostered by advanced technologies including scientific visualization, online communities, digital video collaboratories, and wireless handheld computers. Much of this work concerns aspects of computational thinking on the part of tool users. His current work is developing a new paradigm for everyday networked video interactions for learning and communications, and for how informal and formal learning can be better understood and connected, as co-principal investigator of the LIFE Center funded by the National Science Foundation as one of several large-scale national

Science of Learning Centers. He is co-editor of the 2007 volume *Video Research in the Learning Sciences*. He was co-author of the 2000 National Research Council volume *How People Learn*. Pea founded and served as the first director of the learning sciences doctoral programs at Northwestern University (1991) and Stanford University (2001). He is a fellow of the National Academy of Education, the Association for Psychological Science, the Center for Advanced Study in the Behavioral Sciences, and the American Educational Research Association. In 2004-2005, he was president of the International Society for the Learning Sciences.

Mitchel Resnick, a professor of Learning Research at the MIT Media Laboratory, develops new technologies to engage people (especially children) in creative learning experiences. His research group developed the "programmable bricks" that were the basis for the LEGO MindStorms robotics construction kits. Resnick co-founded the Computer Clubhouse project, an international network of after-school learning centers for youth from low-income communities. Resnick's group recently developed a new programming language, called Scratch, which makes it easier for children to create their own interactive stories, games, and animations—and to share their creations on the Web. In the process, children learn to think creatively, reason systematically, and work collaboratively. He worked for 5 years as a science and technology journalist for *Business Week* magazine, and he has consulted around the world on the uses of new technologies in education. Resnick earned a B.S. in physics from Princeton University, and an M.S. and a Ph.D. in computer science from MIT.

Eric Roberts is a professor of computer science at Stanford University and past chair of the ACM Education Board. His research focuses on computer science education, and is he the author of five textbooks that have been used widely throughout the world. From 1998 to 2005, Roberts was principal investigator for the Bermuda Project, which developed the computer science curriculum for Bermuda's public secondary schools. Roberts has also been active in professional organizations dedicated to computer science education. From 2005 to 2007, he served as co-chair of the Education Board of the Association for Computing Machinery (ACM) and was for many years on the board of the ACM Special Interest Group on Computer Science Education (SIGCSE). From 1998 to 2001, Roberts served as co-chair and principal editor for the ACM/IEEE CS Joint Task Force on Computing Curricula 2001, which published a detailed set of curriculum guidelines in December 2001. He also chaired the ACM Java Task Force from 2004 to 2006. In 2003, Roberts received the SIGCSE Award for Outstanding Contribution to Computer Science Education. Professor Roberts is a fellow of the ACM and the American Association for the

Advancement of Science. He received his A.B., M.S., and Ph.D. degrees in applied mathematics from Harvard University.

Robert Sproull is a vice president and fellow at Sun Microsystems. He founded and led the Massachusetts branch of Sun Microsystems Laboratories for more than 10 years and is currently serving as interim director of Sun Microsystems Laboratories. Since undergraduate days, he has been building hardware and software for computer graphics: clipping hardware, an early device-independent graphics package, page description languages, laser printing software, and window systems. He has also been involved in VLSI design, especially of asynchronous circuits and systems. Before joining Sun in 1990, he was a principal with Sutherland, Sproull & Associates, an associate professor at Carnegie Mellon University, and a member of the Xerox Palo Alto Research Center. He is a coauthor with William Newman of the early text *Principles of Interactive Computer Graphics*. He is an author of the recently published book *Logical Effort*, which deals with designing fast CMOS circuits. Sproull was elected in 1997 to the National Academy of Engineering for his work in computer graphics and digital printing. He is a fellow of the American Academy of Arts and Sciences and has served on the U.S. Air Force Scientific Advisory Board. Sproull received a B.A in physics from Harvard College in 1968, and an M.S. and a Ph.D. in computer science from Stanford University, in 1970 and 1977.

Gerald Jay Sussman is the Panasonic (formerly Matsushita) Professor of Electrical Engineering at the Massachusetts Institute of Technology. Since 1964, he has worked on artificial intelligence research at MIT. He has also worked in computer languages and in computer architecture and VLSI design. Using the Digital Orrery he designed, Sussman has worked with Jack Wisdom to discover numerical evidence for chaotic motions in the outer planets. Sussman is coauthor (with Hal Abelson and Julie Sussman) of the introductory computer science textbook used at MIT from 1985 through 2007. The textbook (Harold Abelson, Gerald Jay Sussman, and Julie Sussman, 1985, *Structure and Interpretation of Computer Programs*, 1st edition, Cambridge, Mass., MIT Press) has been translated into French, German, Polish, Chinese, and Japanese. Sussman has pioneered the use of computational descriptions to communicate methodological ideas in teaching subjects in electrical circuits and in signals and systems. Over the past decade Sussman and Wisdom have developed a subject that uses computational techniques to communicate a deeper understanding of advanced classical mechanics. Computational algorithms are used to express the methods used in the analysis of dynamical phenomena. Expressing the methods in a computer language forces them to be unambiguous and computationally effective. Sussman and Wisdom, with Meinhard Mayer, have produced a textbook, *Structure and Interpretation of Classical Mechanics*, to capture these ideas. Sussman is a fellow of the Institute of Electrical and Electronics Engineers. He is a member of the National Academy of Engineering and is also a fellow of the American Association for the Advancement of Science, the American Association for Artificial Intelligence, the Association for Computing Machinery (ACM), the American Academy of Arts and Sciences, and the New York Academy of Sciences. He received his S.B. and Ph.D. in mathematics from the Massachusetts Institute of Technology in 1968 and 1973, respectively.

Jeannette M. Wing is the President's Professor of Computer Science in the Computer Science Department at Carnegie Mellon University. She received her S.B., S.M., and Ph.D. from the Massachusetts Institute of Technology. From 2004-2007, she was head of the Computer Science Department at Carnegie Mellon. Currently on leave from CMU, she is the assistant director of the Computer and Information Science and Engineering Directorate at the National Science Foundation. Wing's general research interests are in the areas of specification and verification, concurrent and distributed systems, programming languages, and software engineering. Her current focus is on the foundations of trustworthy computing, with specific interests in security and privacy. She published a viewpoint article in the March 2006 issue of *Communications of the Association for Computing Machinery* entitled "Computational Thinking."

Ursula Wolz is the College of New Jersey (TCNJ) Associate Professor of Computer Science and Interactive Multimedia. Wolz is also the principal investigator for the NSF Broadening Participation in Computing via Community Journalism for Middle Schoolers program, and she was the principal investigator of a Microsoft Research project on multidisciplinary game development. She is a recognized computer science educator with a broad range of publications who has taught students including disabled children, urban teachers, and elite undergraduates for more than 30 years. She is a co-founder of the Interactive Multimedia Program at TCNJ. She has a background in computational linguistics, with a Ph.D. in computer science from Columbia University, a master's degree in computing in education from Columbia Teachers College, and a bachelor's degree from MIT, where she was part of Seymour Papert's Logo group at the very beginning of research on constructivist computing environments.

Wm. A. Wulf is a computer scientist notable for his work in programming languages and compilers. As of 2007, he is a professor at the University of Virginia. Wulf's research has included computer architecture, computer security, and hardware-software codesign. While at Carnegie Mellon University, he designed the BLISS programming language and developed a groundbreaking optimizing compiler for it. Wulf is a former president of the National Academy of Engineering and has previously chaired the Computer Science and Telecommunications Board of the National Research Council. He serves on the Council of the ACM and is a reviewing editor of *Science*. In 1994 he was inducted as a fellow of the ACM. In 1993, Wulf was elected to the National Academy of Engineering for professional leadership and for contributions to programming systems and computer architecture. He attended the University of Illinois, receiving a B.S. in engineering physics and an M.S. in electrical engineering, and then achieved a Ph.D. in computer science from the University of Virginia.

B.3 STAFF

Herbert S. Lin, the study director, is chief scientist for the National Research Council's Computer Science and Telecommunications Board, where he has been a study director for major projects on public policy and information technology. These studies include a 1996 study on national cryptography policy (*Cryptography's Role in Securing the Information Society*), a 1991 study on the future of computer science (*Computing the Future*), a 1999 study of Defense Department systems for command, control, communications, computing, and intelligence (*Realizing the Potential of C4I: Fundamental Challenges*), a 2000 study on workforce issues in high technology (*Building a Workforce for the Information Economy*), a 2002 study on protecting kids from Internet pornography and sexual exploitation (*Youth, Pornography, and the Internet*), a 2004 study on aspects of the FBI's information technology modernization program (*A Review of the FBI's Trilogy IT Modernization Program*), a 2005 study on electronic voting (*Asking the Right Questions About Electronic Voting*), a 2005 study on computational biology (*Catalyzing Inquiry at the Interface of Computing and Biology*), a 2007 study on privacy and information technology (*Engaging Privacy and Information Technology in a Digital Age*), a 2007 study on cybersecurity research (*Toward a Safer and More Secure Cyberspace*), a 2009 study on health care information technology (*Computational Technology for Effective Health Care*), and a 2009 study on cyberattack (*Technology, Policy, Law, and Ethics Regarding U.S. Acquisition and Use of Cyberattack Capabilities*). Before his NRC service, he was a professional staff member and staff scientist for the House Armed Services Committee (1986-1990), where his portfolio included defense policy and arms control issues. He received his doctorate in physics from MIT. Apart from his CSTB work, he is published in cognitive science, science education, biophysics, and arms control and defense policy. He also consults on K-12 math and science education.

Enita A. Williams is an associate program officer with the Computer Science and Telecommunications Board of the National Research Council. She formerly served as a research associate for the Air Force Studies Board of the National Academies where she supported a number of projects, including a standing committee for the Special Operations Command (SOCOM) and standing committee for the intelligence community (TIGER). Prior to her work at the National Academies, she served as a program assistant with the Scientific Freedom, Responsibility and Law Program of AAAS, where she drafted the human enhancement workshop report. Ms. Williams graduated from Stanford University with a B.A. in public policy with a focus on science and technology policy, and an M.A. in communications.

C

Executive Summary from *Being Fluent with Information Technology*

Information technology is playing an increasingly important role in the work and personal lives of citizens. Computers, communications, digital information, software—the constituents of the information age—are everywhere.

Between those who search aggressively for opportunities to learn more about information technology and those who choose not to learn anything at all about information technology, there are many who recognize the potential value of information technology for their everyday lives and who realize that a better understanding of information technology will be helpful to them. This realization is based on several factors:

- Information technology has entered our lives over a relatively brief period of time with little warning and essentially no formal educational preparation for most people.
- Many who currently use information technology have only a limited understanding of the tools they use and a (probably correct) belief that they are underutilizing them.
- Many citizens do not feel confident or in control when confronted by information technology, and they would like to be more certain of themselves.
- There have been impressive claims for the potential benefits of information technology, and many would like to realize those benefits.

NOTE: Reprinted from National Research Council, 1999, *Being Fluent with Information Technology*, Washington, D.C.: National Academy Press, pp. 1-5.

APPENDIX C

- There is concern on the part of some citizens that changes implied by information technology embody potential risks to social values, freedoms or economic interests, etc., obligating them to become informed.

And, naturally, there is simple curiosity about how this powerful and pervasive technology works.

These various motivations to learn more about information technology raise the general question, What should everyone know about information technology in order to use it more effectively now and in the future? Addressing that question is the subject of this report.

The answer to this question is complicated by the fact that information technology is changing rapidly. The electronic computer is just over 50 years old, "PC," as in personal computer, is less than 20 years old, and the World Wide Web has been known to the public for less than five years. In the presence of rapid change, it is impossible to give a fixed, once-and-for-all course that will remain current and effective.

Generally, "computer literacy" has acquired a "skills" connotation, implying competency with a few of today's computer applications, such as word processing and e-mail. Literacy is too modest a goal in the presence of rapid change, because it lacks the necessary "staying power." As the technology changes by leaps and bounds, existing skills become antiquated and there is no migration path to new skills. A better solution is for the individual to plan to adapt to changes in the technology. This involves learning sufficient foundational material to enable one to acquire new skills independently after one's formal education is complete.

This requirement of a deeper understanding than is implied by the rudimentary term "computer literacy" motivated the committee to adopt "fluency" as a term connoting a higher level of competency. People fluent with information technology (FIT persons) are able to express themselves creatively, to reformulate knowledge, and to synthesize new information. Fluency with information technology (i.e., what this report calls FITness) entails a process of lifelong learning in which individuals continually apply what they know to adapt to change and acquire more knowledge to be more effective at applying information technology to their work and personal lives.

Fluency with information technology requires three kinds of knowledge: contemporary skills, foundational concepts, and intellectual capabilities. These three kinds of knowledge prepare a person in different ways for FITness.

- Contemporary skills, the ability to use today's computer applications, enable people to apply information technology immediately. In the present labor market, skills are an essential component of job readiness. Most importantly, skills provide a store of practical experience on which to build new competence.
- Foundational concepts, the basic principles and ideas of computers, networks, and information, underpin the technology. Concepts

explain the how and why of information technology, and they give insight into its opportunities and limitations. Concepts are the raw material for understanding new information technology as it evolves.

• Intellectual capabilities, the ability to apply information technology in complex and sustained situations, encapsulate higher-level thinking in the context of information technology. Capabilities empower people to manipulate the medium to their advantage and to handle unintended and unexpected problems when they arise. The intellectual capabilities foster more abstract thinking about information and its manipulation.

For specificity, the report enumerates the ten highest-priority items for each of the three types of knowledge. (Box ES.1 lists these ten items for each type of knowledge.) The skills, linked closely to today's computer usage, will change over time, but the concepts and capabilities are timeless.

Concepts, capabilities, and skills—the three different types of knowledge of FITness—occupy separate dimensions, implying that a particular activity involving information technology will involve elements of each type of knowledge. Learning the skills and concepts and developing the intellectual capabilities can be undertaken without reference to each other, but such an effort will not promote FITness to any significant degree. The three elements of FITness are co-equal, each reinforcing the others, and all are essential to FITness.

FITness is personal in the sense that individuals fluent with information technology evaluate, distinguish, learn, and use new information technology as appropriate to their own personal and professional activities. What is appropriate for an individual depends on the particular applications, activities, and opportunities for being FIT that are associated with the individual's area of interest or specialization.

FITness is also graduated and dynamic. It is graduated in the sense that FITness is characterized by different levels of sophistication (rather than a single fluent/not fluent judgment). And, it is dynamic in that FITness entails lifelong learning as information technology evolves.

In short, FITness should not be regarded as an end state that is independent of domain, but rather as something that develops over a lifetime in particular domains of interest and that has a different character and tone depending on which domains are involved. Accordingly, the pedagogic goal is to provide students with a sufficiently complete foundation of the three types of knowledge that they can "learn the rest of it" on their own as the need arises throughout life.

Because FITness is fundamentally integrative, calling upon an individual to coordinate information and skills with respect to multiple dimensions of a problem and to make overall judgments and decisions taking all such information into account, a project-based approach to developing FITness is most appropriate. Projects of appropriate scale and scope inherently involve multiple iterations, each of which provides an opportunity for an instructional checkpoint or intervention. The domain

BOX ES.1
The Components of Fluency with Information Technology

Intellectual Capabilities

1. Engage in sustained reasoning.
2. Manage complexity.
3. Test a solution.
4. Manage problems in faulty solutions.
5. Organize and navigate information structures and evaluate information.
6. Collaborate.
7. Communicate to other audiences.
8. Expect the unexpected.
9. Anticipate changing technologies.
10. Think about information technology abstractly.

Information Technology Concepts

1. Computers
2. Information systems
3. Networks
4. Digital representation of information
5. Information organization
6. Modeling and abstraction
7. Algorithmic thinking and programming
8. Universality
9. Limitations of information technology
10. Societal impact of information and information technology

Information Technology Skills

1. Setting up a personal computer
2. Using basic operating system features
3. Using a word processor to create a text document
4. Using a graphics and/or an artwork package to create illustrations, slides, or other image-based expressions of ideas
5. Connecting a computer to a network
6. Using the Internet to find information and resources
7. Using a computer to communicate with others
8. Using a spreadsheet to model simple processes or financial tables
9. Using a database system to set up and access useful information
10. Using instructional materials to learn how to use new applications or features

of a project can be tailored to an individual's interest (e.g., in the department of a student's major), thereby providing motivation for a person to expend the (non-trivial) effort to master the concepts and skills of FITness. In addition, a project of appropriate scope will be sufficiently complex that intellectual integration is necessary to complete it. Note also that much of the infrastructure of existing skills-based computer or information technology literacy efforts (e.g., hardware, software, network connections, support staff) will be important elements of efforts to promote FITness.

Although the essentials of FITness are for the most part not dependent on sophisticated mathematics, and should therefore generally be accessible in some form to every citizen, any program or effort to make individuals more FIT must be customized to the target population. Because the committee was composed of college and university faculty, the committee chose to focus its implementational concerns on the four-year college or university graduate as one important starting point for the development of FITness across the citizenry. Further, the committee believes that successful implementation of FITness instruction will requires serious rethinking of the college and university curriculum. It will not be sufficient for individual instructors to revisit their course content or approach. Rather, entire departments must examine the question of the extent to which their students will graduate FIT. Universities need to concern themselves with the FITness of students who cross discipline boundaries and with the extent to which each discipline is meeting the goals of universal FITness.

In summary, FIT individuals, those who know a starter set of IT skills, who understand the basic concepts on which IT is founded, and who have engaged in the higher-level thinking embodied in the intellectual capabilities, should use information technology confidently, should come to work ready to learn new business systems quickly and use them effectively, should be able to apply IT to personally relevant problems, and should be able to adapt to the inevitable change as IT evolves over their lifetime. To be FIT is to possess knowledge essential to using information technology now and in the future.

D

Supplemental Bibliography

Barron, Brigid. 2006. "Interest and Self-Sustained Learning as Catalysts of Development: A Learning Ecology Perspective." *Human Development* 49:193-224.

Bell, Philip. 2005. "Reflections on the Cognitive and Social Foundations of Information and Communication Technology Fluency." Paper read at Workshop on ICT Fluency and High School Graduation Outcomes, October 23-24, 2005, Washington, D.C.

Bell, Tim, Ian H. Witten, and Mike Fellows. 2006. *Computer Science Unplugged: An Enrichment and Extension Programme for Primary-Aged Children*. Canterbury, New Zealand: Computer Science Unplugged.

Blikstein, Paulo, and Uri Wilensky. 2007. "Bifocal Modeling: A Framework for Combining Computer Modeling, Robotics and Real-World Sensing." Paper presented at the annual meeting of the American Educational Research Association (AERA 2007), April 9-13, 2007, Chicago.

Blum, Lenore, and Thomas J. Cortina. 2007. "CS4HS: An Outreach Program for High School CS Teachers." Paper read at ACM Special Interest Group on Computer Science Education, March 7-10, 2007, Covington, Kentucky.

Blum, Lenore, and Richard J. Lipton. 2009. "Algorithms: Tiny Yet Powerful—and We Can't Live Without Them." Available at http://rjlipton.wordpress.com/2009/02/13/algorithms-tiny-yet-powerful/.

Carnegie Mellon University, Center for Computational Thinking. See http://www.cs.cmu.edu/~CompThink/.

Denning, Peter. 2004. "Great Principles in Computing Curricula." Paper read at ACM Special Interest Group on Computer Science Education, March 3-7, 2004, Norfolk, Virginia.

Denning, Peter. 2009. "Beyond Computational Thinking: A CACM IT Profession Column." *Communications of the ACM* 52(6):28-30.

diSessa, Andrea. 2008. "Can Students Re-Invent Fundamental Scientific Principles?: Evaluating the Promise of New-Media Literacies." In *Children's Learning in a Digital World*, edited by T. Willoughby and E. Wood. Oxford, United Kingdom: Blackwell Publishing.

diSessa, Andrea. 2005. "Systemics of Learning for a Revised Pedagogical Agenda." In *Foundations for the Future in Mathematics Education*, edited by R. Lesh. Mahwah, New Jersey: Lawrence Erlbaum Associates.
Glass, Robert L. 2006. "Call It Problem Solving, Not Computational Thinking." *Communications of the ACM* 49(9):13.
Goldman, Shelley, Roy Pea, Heidy Maldonado, Lee Martin, Toby White, and WILD Team of Stanford University. 2004. "Functioning in the Wireless Classroom." Paper read at 2nd IEEE International Workshop on Wireless and Mobile Technologies in Education (WMTE '04), March 23-25, 2004, Washington, D.C.
Goldman, Shelley, Roy Pea, Heidy Maldonado, and WILD Team of Stanford University. 2004. "Emerging Social Engineering in the Wireless Classroom." Paper read at International Conference on Learning Sciences, Proceedings of the 6th International Conference on Learning Sciences, June 22-26, 2004, Santa Monica, Calif.
Hazzan, Orit, Judith Gal-Ezer, and Lenore Blum. 2008. "A Model for High School Computer Science Education: The Four Key Elements That Make It!" Paper read at SIGCSE 2008, March 12-15, Portland, Oregon.
Kay, Alan. 2005. "Squeak Etoys, Children & Learning." In *Viewpoints Research Institute, VPRI Research Note RN-2005-001*. Available at http://www.vpri.org/pdf/rn2005001_learning.pdf.
Levy, Sharona T., and David Mioduser. 2008. "Does It 'Want' or 'Was It Programmed to'. . .? Kindergarten Children's Explanations of an Autonomous Robot's Adaptive Functioning." *International Journal of Technology and Design Education* 18:337-359.
Moursund, Dave. 2006. *Computational Thinking and Math Maturity: Improving Math Education in K-8 Schools*. Eugene, Oregon: University of Oregon Press.
National Research Council. 1999. *Being Fluent with Information Technology*. Washington, D.C.: National Academy Press.
National Research Council. 2004. "The Essential Character of Computer Science." In *Computer Science: Reflections on the Field, Reflections from the Field*. Washington, D.C.: The National Academies Press.
National Research Council. 2004. "The Legacy of Computer Science." In *Computer Science: Reflections on the Field, Reflections from the Field*. Washington, D.C.: The National Academies Press.
National Research Council. 2005. "ICT Fluency and High Schools: A Workshop Summary." Paper read at Workshop on ICT Fluency and High School Graduation Outcomes, October 23-24, 2005, Washington, D.C.
Phillps, Pat. 2007. Presentation: "Computational Thinking: A Problem-Solving Tool for Every Classroom." Microsoft. Available at http://www.cs.cmu.edu/~CompThink/resources/ct_pat_phillips.pdf.
Resnick, Mitchel, John Maloney, Andrés Monroy Hernández, Natalie Rusk, Evelyn Eastmond, Karen Brennan, Amon Millner, Eric Rosenbaum, Jay Silver, Brian Silverman, and Yasmin Kafai. 2009. "Scratch: Programming for All." *Communications of the ACM* 52(11):60-67.
SECANT: Science Education in Computational Thinking, Purdue University, http://secant.cs.purdue.edu/.
Stonedahl, Forrest, Michelle Wilkerson-Jerde, and Uri Wilensky. 2009. "Re-conceiving Introductory Computer Science Curricula Through Agent-Based Modeling." *Proceedings of the EduMAS Workshop at AAMAS 2009*. Evanston, Illinois: Center for Connected Learning and Computer-Based Modeling, Northwestern University.
Sysło, Maciej M., and Anna Beata Kwiatkowska. 2008. "The Challenging Face of Informatics Education in Poland." Paper read at Informatics Education—Supporting Computational Thinking: Third International Conference on Informatics in Secondary Schools—Evolution and Perspectives, July, Torun, Poland.

Wing, Jeannette M. 2008. "Computational Thinking and Thinking About Computing." *Philosophical Transactions of the Royal Society A* 366:3717-3725.
Wing, Jeannette M. 2008. "Five Deep Questions in Computing." *Communications of the ACM* 51(1):58-60.